## BEING A WOMAN IS FANTASTIC!

Here is a cheer for all the women who have stayed in there, fulfilled and happy as women, wives, mothers, sometimes with careers as well, but always maintaining the basic moral truths that never change. For we truly know that a woman's greatest gift is to share these special principles—these truths that hold the universe together. Sometimes we don't express them openly, but they are always there, and we think the time has come for them to be revealed, renewed, supported and praised.

## WHAT EVERY WOMAN *STILL* KNOWS

"Millie Cooper and Martha Fanning have written a book that today's woman has long been looking for. Their book is presented in the warm and friendly manner of two women who really care about other women and who want to share what they hold dear."

—Mrs. Tom Landry

# What Every Woman Still Knows

### A Celebration of The Christian Liberated Woman

## Mildred Cooper
## Martha Janning

BANTAM BOOKS · TORONTO · NEW YORK · LONDON

WHAT EVERY WOMAN STILL KNOWS

*A Bantam Book/published by arrangement with
M. Evans and Company, Inc.*

PRINTING HISTORY
*Evans edition published October 1978
2nd printing . . . January 1979
Bantam edition/June 1979*

## ACKNOWLEDGMENTS

Thanks are due to the following publishers for permission
to use previously copyrighted material:

Harcourt Brace Jovanovich, Inc. for lines from *E. E. Cummings: A Miscellany*, edited by George Firmage. Reprinted by permission of Harcourt Brace Jovanovich, Inc.

Holt, Rinehart and Winston for lines from "The Death of the Hired Man" from *The Poetry of Robert Frost*, edited by Edward Connery Lathem. Copyright 1930, 1939, © 1969 by Holt, Rinehart and Winston, Copyright © 1958 by Robert Frost. Copyright © 1967 by Leslie Frost Ballantine. Reprinted by permission of Holt, Rinehart and Winston, Publishers.

Tyndale House Publishers for verses from *The Living Bible*. Copyright 1971 by Tyndale House Publishers. Used by permission.

Sequoia-Elsevier Publishing Co., Inc. for lines from "The Morning Walk" from *Now We Are Six* by A. A. Milne. Copyright 1927 by E. P. Dutton; renewal © 1955 by A. A. Milne. Reprinted by permission of the publishers, E. P. Dutton.

*Dedicated with our fervent love*
*to Ken and Buckner—*
*who have shared in it all,*
*who have affirmed us all the way,*
*and who, through their love over the years,*
*have made our marriages and our being women*
*a joy beyond words!*

These acknowledgments are very significant for they reflect the people who believed in us enough to cause this book to materialize—so we very happily and gratefully thank: Herb Katz, who believed in us and what we "know," who believed we had company in this "knowing," who first suggested that we put it all down, and who wonderfully challenged us with his marvelous enthusiasm; Joyce Christmas, whose invaluable suggestions and hours of editorial counsel not only constantly reinforced our confidence, but also created a wonderful friendship that we will always cherish; Pam Veley, whose genuine interest and most capable editorial assistance continually encouraged us through the many months; Carmen Garcia, whose love and caring about this book resulted in her ear being bent hours on end and her opinions being genuinely valued; Marianne Housman, who typed and typed and typed, and kept encouraging words coming along with her supremely gracious attitude; our children, Berkley, Tyler, Lisa, Mike, and Steve, who were encouraging and patient beyond description as they heard and said over and over for more than a year, "Wait just a minute, Mother's working on the book!"; Steve Fanning, who conceptualized the book beautifully in a photograph he made as a gift for his mother, and which, to his surprise, became the cover of the book; and to all of our dear interested friends who shared and listened, contributed and encouraged—we hope we've crystalized what you know and hold dear—we love you and thank you.

# Introduction

## Letting the World in on a Secret

Every book ought to have a good reason to be! A really good reason. Whether you're reading it for fun or philosophy, it should somehow enrich your life and not waste those hours given to it. Hours are precious.

We think this book has as good a reason as can be—it's our open letter to the world, some warm and tender feelings, about some remarkable secrets almost all women share down deep inside. These secrets are actually the glue that holds the universe together. Often they aren't expressed openly, but they are always there, and we think the time has come for them to be revealed, renewed, supported, and praised. We hope you'll find something *you* hold dear crystallized here, for you who have stood by these truths steadfastly ought to know that you're not alone—you are part of the multitude.

This multitude is made up of a lot of remarkable women. Often they're so busy going about the business of living fulfilled, satisfying, and challenging lives that no one hears very much about them or how they think and feel. They either feel that everyone is living the same way or—thanks to the spotlighting of weird and reactionary fringes of society by the media—that no one is! Sometimes they feel alone, most of the time they don't press for attention, yet they have more value and reality for our world than any name or movement that flashes into the headlines today and is gone tomorrow.

A satisfying, comfortably spontaneous lifestyle, free in the knowledge of the love of God, strengthened beyond measure by a sure belief in certain moral absolutes that never change is just that—*satisfying*, and adventuresome and exciting! The cynics and the moral free-floaters can't seem to believe such lives exist. They deny it, claiming to speak for everyone. Nonsense.

But before you jump to the conclusion that the multitude we're speaking about have no problems or that they're Pollyannas heading up peaceful little kingdoms, wait a minute. No one ever said that a fulfilled life is simple or easy or not bought at a price. Real spiritual quality is not brought about instantly, but is wrought out daily, with hard work, love, concern—and real effort. Spiritual conversion is an instantaneous new beginning, a new direction in Jesus Christ, but quality spiritual living is a daily task, concerned with every minute detail of the "day-*in*-ness" and "day-*out*-ness" of life. Because God is concerned—

Oh Lord, You have examined my heart and know everything about me. You know when I sit or stand. When far away You know my every thought. You chart the path ahead of me, and tell me where to stop and rest. Every moment, You know where I am. You know what I am going to say before I even say it. You both precede and follow me, and place Your hand of blessing on my head. *(Psalms 139:1–5)*

What a difference that makes! And what a grand challenge! It's not the free-floating, directionless existence of the cynic; that kind of life-style is a cop-out. The challenge of spiritual quality in life demands the noblest and best effort, total courage, and your all, your very self, for that's what God gave us—His all, Himself. This grand spiritual journey was bought primarily with *the* price of His Son, Jesus Christ; and it is costly and priceless to the multitude.

What needs to be crystallized, then, what secrets need to be expressed, what kind of glue is it that holds all this together? It's going to be fun throughout this book to lead a cheer for all the women who've stayed in there, being fulfilled and happy as women, wives, mothers—sometimes with careers as well, but always maintaining the basic moral absolutes that *never* change. There is no challenge on earth like shaping the character of a child, no more satisfying knowledge than the awareness that the strength of any nation lies in the strength of its homes. Only mothers can "mother," and being a woman is fantastic! These are the secrets we want to talk about.

We know that there are multitudes of women who *still* know and act on these strong principles. They are totally satisfied and challenged—not threatened by ultra-feminists or ultra-doormats. Neither of those manipulative roles is necessary for the fulfilled woman. Sure, she can learn from theories and trends, and she can determine what is cheap or what is unnecessary for her. Remember that extremes of either kind—the obviously aggressive or the fakely submissive—indicate real insecurity in a woman, not fulfillment. An exciting principle goes into effect here. God has a way of honoring and reassuring those who honor His laws, be they physical or spiritual.

The person who obeys the law of gravity ends up with fewer broken bones than the one who says it doesn't exist. In exactly the same way, the person who unswervingly believes in and obeys God's spiritual laws of right and wrong has a spiritual health. How stupid ever to think that God, who is Spirit, put more teeth into His physical laws than into His spiritual laws. It's a generous and foolish game that a lot of so-called intelligent people play. As Alexander Solzhenitsyn said: "If we are deprived of the concepts of good and evil, what will be left? Nothing but the manipulation of one another. We will sink to the status of animals."

What's the big secret, then? Here it is: In spite of what we're fed by the media and the loud voices predicting doom, in spite of all the revolutionary movements and the changes we see happening around us, there are still multitudes who have listened, do listen, will continue to listen to that reassuring "still, small Voice" of God as the director and patterner of their lives. It is these multitudes who have never given up their strong commitment to moral absolutes, that have shared a wonderful secret, a secret of stability, a secret of order, a secret knowledge that without them this country, this world would have surely fallen apart.

They have always known it; they *still* know it. And we're setting about in this book to say, "Amen!"

The Lord grants good sense to the godly—His

saints. He shows how to distinguish right from wrong, how to find the right decision every time.

The man who knows right from wrong and has good judgment and common sense is happier than the man who is immensely rich! For such wisdom is far more valuable than precious jewels. Nothing else compares with it. *(Proverbs 2:7–9 and 3:13–15)*

# One

# The Book Every Woman Wishes She Could Write

In the years we've known each other, the two of us have often talked about how exciting it would be to write a book together. A book about the one thing we know best—what it means to be a woman in a time when the lives of ordinary women like us are being changed because our society is changing—based upon what we've experienced. A book that highlights those values that never change, that affirms the strong support our faith has given us, that tells the real and wonderful joys of being wives and mothers, and shares the challenges and excitement of really relating to people we meet and work with outside the home. We would try very hard to write in a way that would illuminate and inspire, give joy in a world that so desperately needs it, and encouragement, under-

1

standing, and hope in a world that sometimes seems very, very lonely and confusing.

Then we're brought back to earth. Isn't that a book every woman could write? All those things we think about living, working, surviving, about marriage and children, happiness and grief—are things every woman knows. Has always known. Will still know years from now, even when politics and movements and revolutions have had their say and had their day.

But wait a minute. There's one point that a lot of women today seem to have forgotten, or perhaps have not thought about at all. Whether they are young and untried, or worldly and sophisticated, married, single, homemakers, career women, city or country dwellers, that strong, eternal sense of "knowing" that we're talking about makes women's lives simply different from men's—not better, not worse, only different. It is a difference beautifully ordained by God and nature, a difference that has a purpose.

This difference in our lives is possibly the most important quality we women bring to the world, and it should be celebrated! We need to realize that it was set into motion by God to work *for* us and our loved ones, and we should delight in our special uniqueness. Our eyes do not see what happens in just the same way our husbands, fathers, and sons perceive events, nor do our minds interpret *all* of life's experiences in exactly the same way. Our roles as men and women are not identical because our lives have different centers. And that's good.

Oh, you might say, there's no such thing anymore. It's a unisex world, isn't it? No, not at all. There'll always be a difference—and should be—regardless of equal job opportunities, equal pay, or what have you. Nature backs that—life backs it—for it's set in motion by God Himself. There is a distinct man's world where he flourishes and has been equipped to; likewise women have their equally meaningful and essential gifts and their world. Where these worlds meet, and they're meeting more and more both in business and in home responsibilities, there's supposed to be a strong blending of talents, not an erasing of one for the other. Why compete? There's no earthly or heavenly reason to. In Lisa Sergio's magnificent book, *Jesus and Woman*, she writes: "The strength of any partnership lies in the diversity of its partners, whose different attributes, complementing each other, contribute to the formation of a complete, or more nearly complete, whole. Being equal is not synonymous with being identical." She goes on eloquently to say that, "the logical fact is that if woman had nothing different to contribute to the management of human affairs than what it already receives from man, her participation would be neither interesting nor necessary." Powerful and true.

We believe that this difference is essential for our dignity as women and that a comfortable and even gratifying feeling about it is necessary for contentment and fulfillment. Whether we want to be successful and happy homemakers or the president of a corporation or both, we have to learn better how to draw on what we know as women. It is profitless to devote our lives to rejecting or ignoring what exists; but there is immense profit and wisdom to be gained by accepting what exists. *within* us—what every woman *still* knows.

There are vast and sundry meanings contained in that simple phrase, and none of them are simple. We "know" certain things instinctively, intuitively, about being a woman. A twelve-year-old girl knows them as well as an eighty-year-old grandmother. But the sixty years between them are really a long process

3

of discovering just what it is that we do know. We gradually learn to recognize and understand our gifts and our power. We make mistakes, of course, and sometimes it's hard to pin down our errors, for we deal so often in intangibles, in things that are sensed and not seen, rather than "products." The manufacturer of a new model car can quickly tell by sales figures whether or not he's made a mistake, but the mother of a troubled teen-ager or the wife in a troubled marriage doesn't have it so easy. What went wrong? Who went wrong and why? She wonders and analyzes and seeks answers. Facing that kind of challenge and heartbreak is a lonely task; there are no written figures against which you can check your calculations, and there are no accountants to point out your errors. We have to draw on what we've learned in the past and depend on our inner strength. No book can tell you what to do. It can only tell you what others have done, suggest ways of applying the special abilities all women are born with, and remind you of your enormous strengths and the great and eternal source of strength that is available to all who seek Him, the Lord.

Slowly, as the days and years pass, we learn. What we know as twelve-year-olds is like a tightly rolled bud that promises one day to blossom into a fragrant and beautiful flower. The bud is nourished, encouraged, and cultivated to fullness by the experiences of a lifetime and by women's special, God-given gifts. But we can, if we choose, allow the bud to wither or let the storms of living break it if we haven't learned to protect it with strong supports. The fragrance of the blossom reaches so many people—our husbands, our children, our friends, relatives, even distant people never seen face-to-face. And ourselves. We must never lose sight of our *own* place in our lives, and must be comfortable in that understanding. We need a strong and healthy alliance with ourselves. God ordains this. The Bible tells us that ". . . no man should think more highly of himself *than he ought,*" indicating *that he ought* to be able to think highly of himself—healthfully not vainly. Usually to have self-respect and heap it on others, we have to *be* respectful. In the depths of our conscience, we usually keep private tabs of some sort on ourselves, so having a healthy self-respect is not the free ride it looks. We women who so naturally deal in intangibles know that we must earn it. When we do, we know there's an energy and glow that no cosmetic can produce.

This, then, is the book we would want to write: not just a list of what we all know, but a reminder to all women of how what we know affects our journey through our lives, about how our differences from men are not a weakness but a strength, a necessary strength. And we want to say somethings about the Source of our gifts, about God and His place in our lives, and how He and our inborn abilities can meet and solve problems of marriage, children, and living.

It's sometimes easier to describe a feeling about life by a simple story. There's a true and touching one we both love that describes how we feel about being women, that says so much about all women's lives and our mutual pilgrimage. A loving, dedicated woman went to Africa as a missionary to teach a tribe that had had little contact with the outside world and none with the teachings of Christianity. She lived with them in their poor village on the West African coast and tried to teach them the message of love and faith that Jesus brought to mankind. Some days she had doubts about whether they were really understanding her, and then, once in a while, she could sense that her efforts were succeeding.

A remarkable thing happened one Christmas season. She explained about gifts and how Jesus was God's gift to the world. Deeply touched by this, one young native boy set out on Christmas morning for a spot on the coast fifteen miles away from the village. It was the only place for hundreds of miles where a particularly rare and beautiful shell could be found, and he wanted to find one to give as his gift to the missionary. He made the long journey, found the shell, and walked back to present his gift proudly to the woman.

The woman held the priceless, glowing shell in her hand, and knew the amazing effort he had made. "But you had to go so far for it," she said. "It was such a long walk."

The boy nodded and then said the most profound words: "Long walk—part of gift!"

The long walk that is part of the gift is something women know about life. They understand the walk from its deepest symbolisms like that incredible nine-month walk to the delivery room to those countless miles we walk, like that native boy, Christmas shopping for that special gift for the someone we love too. So "Long walk—part of gift"—that's our language. We women understand how that *does* describe our feeling about life and its long walks.

Our marriages are long walks, and we both give and receive much along the way, but just the doing of it is part of the gift. We know there are times when we don't see the road we're traveling clearly, when there are obstacles, when it would perhaps be easier just to stop. There are problems, illness, emotional crises. But we know, too, that it's not for the sake of some prize at the end of the walk that we continue, but for the pilgrimage itself. It's the worst kind of tragedy, really, when a couple, with only a few

6

months of marriage, decide to quit at the first spat. It's so easy to do nowadays; society and the law make it easier, and more acceptable. Acceptable legally maybe, but not that simple a matter for the human spirit. It never is.

No one ever promised that the walk would be easy, and no one ever said that a woman's life would be neatly defined into a few specific roles. Women have always worn more hats than men, and every woman finds that she has to wear a lot of different hats in her lifetime—or in a day. (Maybe that's why women have traditionally taken to hats so readily.) The big question is not *what* all the hats are, but rather the order in which to wear them. Priorities are something that must be dealt with, and women have a gift of knowing this.

Some days, or at some point in our lives, we may have to put on a hat that sends us out of the home to work, but we must never let that hat take total precedence over the other ones in our closet.

At other times, we may put on a seductive, alluring hat and become a playful lover to our husband, but we have to remember that we have other hats stored away; we can't get along with just this one.

We are organizers, administrators, disciplinarians, mediators, teachers, referees, advocates, cooks, cleaners, breadwinners sometimes, companions, advisers, friends, lovers, and oftentimes we're wives, mothers, and daughters all at the same time. We are repairers of all kinds of broken things from hearts to handlebars. And we have ourselves to look out for as well as others.

Sometimes we are challenged to give up an old hat and try out a new one. But we hate giving up our old hats. We know exactly how they feel, how we look in them; we aren't at all certain that the new one will work out . . . we might want the comfortable old one back again, so we like to know it's available. We don't want to put on some frivolous one so often that it may be taking total precedence over the more meaningful ones. And sometimes, strangely enough, we wear a serious, somber, "no-nonsense" hat so long that our bored family needs the relief of a frivolous one. We must know when to wear what. A new hat is an unknown quantity; maybe it will mess up our hair, maybe someone will laugh at us, maybe no one else is wearing that kind of hat and we'll be conspicuous. Or maybe the new hat is so enticing that we forget all the others. There is a danger in forgetting *all* the others . . . we know that, too.

The truth is, we have to juggle hats without pause. It isn't easy, but there are eternal verities that will support us and give us strength. We women have a special framework from which we work. We have innate abilities to help us through our lives, we are privileged as women to have them. God has favored us in many ways. He's given us marvelous qualities and abilities. We can go a long way, just on these wonderful gifts; they are the things women know about themselves and the way they look at the world. But today, more than ever before, we have to put them to good use. We have to be strong, as women have always been strong, and stronger still with all the new opportunities and choices opening up to us and all the new and more difficult responsibilities we have. We need a mighty framework to make our twentieth- and twenty-first-century lives all they can be.

The framework has been there for two thousand years. It is a spiritual framework that transcends day-to-day living, all those changes of hats, and all our instinctive awareness of our qualities as women.

8

The two of us know that if a woman has a spiritual framework, then she can really touch bottom and enjoy the enormous spontaneity and freedom that comes from knowing she is in safe waters. Real liberation is there for the asking, real strength, a conquering spirit.

A wonderfully powerful affirmation—positive and sure—comes into our lives when we find the perfect spiritual framework that supports us in our imperfect humanity. The Bible teaches us that this is the power and presence of Jesus Christ Himself through His Holy Spirit! To us, this is the truth, and it is our belief in this truth that colors our attitudes and actions, even—or especially—when we stumble and fall, for even with the strength of our faith, we make mistakes, we have acted wrongly, we have faced crises to test the most faithful believer.

"If you know the truth," Jesus said, "the truth shall make you free . . . No man comes unto the Father except by me . . . Anyone who tries any other route is like a thief or a robber."

Maybe we'd like to say, "Hey, wait a minute. Let's not do it that way, let's do it this way," but we can't say it. That was what Christ said, and we have no authority to change it. We did not select the condition of man, we don't make the rules, but we are part of the warp and woof of mankind. We accept His words as truth—in fact we accept Him as the Truth, for He made it clear when He said, "I am the Truth." Therefore, we accept His words as truth and the framework they represent is our framework.

Once there was a vertical relationship between man and God that was broken way back yonder, whether we like it or not, by sin. We have a consciousness of sin, we know there is a falling short in us, that there is a need for redemption. And we feel in our hearts the need to return to that vertical relationship

9

with God, some kind of bridge to get back to Him, to reconcile ourselves to Him. We have got to know that we know God and that He knows we are here. That is where our strength comes from.

The bridge is Christ Himself, and every human being needs to find that bridge.

This is our framework, the one the two of us work from, and we believe it is the right one. We have found it to be so, and we rejoice in it!

There comes a time in people's lives when they have to see for themselves who and what they are, really—a spiritual crossroads where they have to decide what this whole thing of living is about. If a person never comes to grips with that question, it's a shallow existence and a frustrating one.

When Nicodemus came to Jesus and asked what he should do, Jesus said, "You have to be born again."

"How do I do that?" Nicodemus asked, genuinely puzzled. "Do I get back into my mother's womb?"

And Jesus said, "You need to be born of the water and the spirit."

Every natural birth is a water birth. The water breaks and the baby comes into the world. The new birth is a spiritual birth. You are born again when you accept Christ as your Savior—you have a spiritual framework. You're no longer dependent on only yourself or on what goes on around you for satisfaction. You have a real knowledge that the Lord is involved in everything that's happening. You know that He is doing things you may not always understand, but you know too that none of us is adequate to deal with all the eternal verities of life.

Once we reach that spiritual crossroads and

have made our choice to follow Jesus, it is the beginning of another long walk, the walk in eternal life.

Jesus said, "When you believe in me, you have eternal life."

Eternal life isn't something that happens when we die. It is a point on our path through *this* life, and when you are born of the spirit, you begin at once to walk in eternal life. And what joy and comfort there is in that! You don't wait and labor through this world, holding your breath, trying to touch bottom, pilgrimaging along and hoping you'll make it until you get to eternal life eventually. It is right there, as soon as you believe. You have it *now*, it's part of the long walk. And that's a powerful something to comprehend, knowing that with each step you take, each decision you make, each pitfall you encounter, you are supported by a strong, eternal framework that inspires your choices, that guides you, that buoys you up when there is absolutely nothing else to cling to.

What has this to do especially with women and what they know? We have said that women deal so often with intangibles, not so much with the gift they can hold and see as with the journey itself. What a comfort it is to know that there is a real framework to sustain you, as positive and concrete as a job description in an office or money in the bank—and a million times more so. Perhaps this is why over the centuries women have been such strong supporters of religion; they perceive quite readily its reality and are able to tap its resources and understand "faith," which the Bible defines as "the evidence of things not seen." Ah, we relate to that, for it speaks to us where we women do so much of our thinking—in our hearts. We can see and feel the form and power of the gifts of the Spirit, just as we can touch the soul of our marriage and

11

come away with a handful of gold instead of empty air.

Not too long ago, our friend Jo Bohannon was at a lovely celebration party for her forty-fifth wedding anniversary. At the dinner, Jo gave as a gift to her husband the following beautiful description of their marriage through her eyes. We thought it such a remarkable gift and such a great picture of the long walk being part of the gift that we wanted to share it with you just as Jo wrote it:

> Ours is not a perfect marriage, but it *is* a good marriage. We never expected it to be anything but a good marriage. Back in 1932, you married for better or for worse (often the case during those Depression years), but mostly you married "for good." And I thought not at all during most of those years of any such thing as terminating our marriage.

> Some might say, "How dull, how unimaginative, how unambitious to be married all one's life to the same person!" I say, "It's just the opposite." In what other relationship do you have the opportunity—and time—to rectify your mistakes, build on your success, work through your problems and decisions, evaluate your progress or lack of it? Oh, it's not easy in a daily, yearly routine; but, oh, it's worth all the effort, the persistent struggle—all the challenge of a lifetime. I believe our love and feelings for one another have enabled us to know each other so much more deeply. It has carried us through the lows of doubt, sorrow, and the shadows and illness in our marriage on to the highs of our good fortune and happiness.

> Marriage must have love to be able to share, to cooperate, and to communicate, to

reach out in an effort to understand another person. We must give, but also forgive, get and sometimes forget but always care and share. At times one must be spouse, child, parent, lover, friend, or even foe. In such a complex environment, it is only love that can keep the relationship from falling apart. I call that love a gift from God. So, if you ask me what every woman still knows, I answer that this woman still knows it's love that makes a marriage a good one. You can call that simply corny or square. I call it simply wonderful!

How readily we and a multitude of women can identify with Jo's words:

Yes, of course. Love and time and effort. Communication, giving, and forgiving. And the lows that come along with the highs—through all these experiences of loving and caring and sharing—in no other relationship do you grow to know another human being quite so completely. It's really remarkable.

It's a lovely, inspiring summary of forty-five years of marriage, isn't it? But someone might say, is it fashionable today, is it still in style? What's so special about it?

To us, it's special because it *is* the life-style of millions of women, many of whom have not been heard from publicly these days, and it's the life millions of other women are searching for. Not all of us have it, not in just the same way, but every woman, we believe, wants the love, the sharing, and the caring that it represents, for she comes equipped with those things to give back. Sure, we can take different roads, experience different life-styles, be successful in all kinds of different fields, but what every woman still knows is that she is most comfortable, most successful when she can fully use all her special qualities, and there is no place quite like marriage and the family for her to do that.

Every woman who has a happy marriage and is sensitive to that counts her blessings and genuinely feels for her friends whose marriages might not be faring so well. That's really true, for when you're as pro-marriage as we are, there's a loss for all when a good thing goes sour. We know our marriages are happy, thank God, but our hearts go out to many of our friends and people we don't even know when things start going on the rocks. In fact, it's some of these unhappy marriages that first started us really thinking about our own.

What we saw in troubled marriages was the destructive pressure of the world in which we live. We saw people slowly disintegrate—their families and their happy home life—not so much because of a third party (that sometimes came much later, if at all), but in the beginning of the trouble, by a kind of creeping paralysis that set in, caused by distorted values and priorities—like addiction to work, the success-syndrome, selling out for social acceptance, and the like. This illness, this lack of ease with one another that is so essential to growth, this "dis-ease" that results in noncommunication, noncommitment, and finally nonexistence for a marriage really troubled us and still does. For we're not insensitive "cloud-sitters" who've never walked in this tough and troubled world. Not on your life. We're human beings, too, who care and understand, live life just like the rest. We do not pretend to know or have all the answers and neither do we pretend that happy marriages are a dime a dozen. We simply care deeply about those going

14

through deep waters and those riding the crest. We do not take marriage in any condition for granted. That's where the trouble starts—taking things for granted—and none of us can be helpful if we don't care.

We realized this "dis-ease" was a kind of poison and it must be treated as such, so we've set about to seek and be aware of antidotes. And we'll be speaking of these in various ways, beginning with the first and foremost—a spiritual base.

Both of us share our common spiritual framework, but we have different talents and opinions. We respect these differences and they have enriched our friendship. We hope to share some of our insights, simply learned and earned over the years of our long walks in marriage, and reassure some women troubled by their life that somebody cares and that all things are possible, that the fact that women have a special way of dealing with the world doesn't make them less of a human being, and that their roles are significant, as much so in the home as in the marketplace. We are not Pollyannas and we'll have none of that sticky sentimentality, we know none of this is easy. We know that there are no simple solutions, but here we have a wonderful opportunity to put down what we honestly believe every woman *still* knows and have our words read by someone who may desire and really hear just what we are sharing. We hope so.

The word *hope* is not used lightly. That's a word everyone of us needs in today's world. So, may we say here, in the spirit of hope, that happy marriages are not all that rare either. We know many of these. A woman from across our country questioned the existence of such a kind of marriage these days. She doubted that it could be. This is a sad reflection on her and the narrow, provincial confines of her life, experiences, and acquaintances. Surely there are troubled marriages, but they are spotlighted today, and we have to work hard to realize that *good* things are as *real* as bad ones. They are, and there are millions of happy marriages to back this up.

They are not like rare hothouse plants either, overcoddled and overanalyzed all the time—there's some of that, but not too much. But in the right soil and surroundings, they grow naturally like orchids in Hawaii. They don't have to be greenhouse grown . . . they're in the right atmosphere. Good marriages are like that. They grow and flower beautifully when the atmosphere is conducive, and the person who doubts this has surely and simply never been exposed.

And so back to that little-big word HOPE. We have lots of hopes for this book, for we've been the recipients ourselves of so many inspiring words—poems, novels, historical documents, accounts of heroism, stories of men and women of destiny who have changed the course of history, of dreamers whose dreams have been realized, words of inspiration, challenge, hope in times of discouragement; the matchless, fathomless words of the Bible, the Word of God, conveyed to us through writers, led by His Spirit, who put down, word for word, the living, vibrant Truth, how to find it and live it, and how to let Him live through us.

We can hope that our words will touch a heart, ease a pain, or at least confirm that what is, is all right. That it is all right to be a woman—wonderfully all right—with all that that entails.

We've said that we have some things in common: our faith and spiritual framework, our happy marriages, and a friendship that goes back many years. But our lives themselves are as different as can be.

The wife of a pastor is surely one of the most challenging jobs in the world, and that is Martha's job. A pastor's wife is an active participant in her husband's work; so many turn to her in times of trouble because she is a woman, and she has many, many opportunities to share with people their deepest concerns. Martha sees this challenge as an honor and she has very deep convictions about her role:

*It's really not quite like any other, I think, for a pastor's wife must really feel the "call," too. You are certainly no "co-pastor," but must sense your best areas of involvement. Your husband is so much to so many people that your understanding sharing of him as well as joining with him is vital. It's about the only role I know of where a woman has a kind of title by which she's always introduced—"the pastor's wife." That's OK, but I've never felt exactly that way about it. I'm not technically "a pastor's wife"—I'm Buckner's wife. He's my husband and my love and that kind of relationship between us really is first. I certainly would pray and do pray to be just exactly the kind of wife he needs as a pastor, for it is a mammoth responsibility he carries, and I so want to be an honor to our wonderful church, too, but I also pray to be that kind of woman he as a man desires—for he is that kind of man to me.*

*. . There are many responsibilities we carry together and separately in a large, growing church. It's a remarkable challenge, one I thank God for, for it's to Him that Buckner and I give our first and greatest allegiance—and together we depend upon Him to help us. There is great comfort in endeavoring to yield our lives to Him—we do better at it sometimes than at others, I'm sure—but we cling to that marvelous promise stated by one of our favorite Christian scholars,*

*Andrew Murray: "God is ready to assume full respon-
sibility for the life wholly yielded to Him." You can't
find anything more reassuring than that!*

In the remarkable church in San Antonio, Trinity Baptist Church, where her husband is pastor, both
he and Martha have shared every human experience
human hearts and lives encounter: joys and sorrows,
marriages and divorces, births and deaths, new
dreams and tarnished ones, blessings and blights,
hopes and disappointments, men and women struggling or strong in their marriages, in their lives at
home or in the world. They have seen their sons, Mike
and Steve, grow to college age and their daughter,
Lisa, about to enter her teen-age years.

Martha made a decision early in her life that
she would not choose a professional career in music,
although the possibility existed, for she had studied
voice since the age of twelve and was awarded two
university scholarships under which she was studying
when she married quite young. She became a wife,
mother, and homemaker first, then continued her vo-
cal studies, singing all the while in the Lord's work,
feeling that the greatest challenge of all.

"Seek ye first the Kingdom of God and His
righteousness and all these things shall be added unto
you."

Martha sings all over the United States and
countless places in the world; she believes in giving
back to God what He gave to her in talent. All things
have been added; there has been no lessening of aspirations or accomplishments by choosing the path she
did. In fact, the added blessings have been over-
whelmingly wonderful. God keeps His word.

Millie's life-style has been different. Her husband, Dr. Kenneth Cooper, developed his pioneering

ideas into a world-famous program of physical fitness called "aerobics." Because he directs the Aerobics Center in Dallas and is a busy physician, author, lecturer, and researcher, she has had to grow into a kind of professional partner, besides being wife, homemaker, and mother of a daughter, Berkley, who, like Martha's Lisa, is nearly a teen-ager, and a son, Tyler, half a dozen years younger. Because both Ken and Millie believe so strongly in aerobics, it has meant that she, too, has become lecturer and author—and that she as well runs four miles a day. She too feels strongly about her role:

*As those of you know who have read the book* Aerobics for Women, *which I co-authored with Ken, there was certainly a time when I was not completely supportive of his work. I loved him dearly but I had not noticed anywhere in the marriage vows where it said I had to run a mile (or four miles) a day in order to be a good wife. But it is difficult if you truly love and admire someone not to become interested in their interests, particularly if they are as all-consuming as Ken's were in the field of physical fitness. As I typed the manuscript for Ken's first book,* Aerobics, *I gradually decided I would give it a try . . . and I have been running ever since. As a result, I started speaking on the subject of exercise whenever Ken was not available and slowly found myself becoming somewhat of a professional speaker. This has enabled Ken and me to travel together as a team all over the world speaking on the subject of physical fitness. This is certainly a fun part of our marriage but by no means the most important—just a nice fringe benefit. You may find this hard to believe, but the real joy in our marriage comes from the daily routine of our lives of living and interacting with our children and friends. We are most contented when we are in our home together as a family. It's still not "fun" to run those four miles; it is "fun" to have become a bit of an expert, to be a co-worker, to be admired by your husband as much as you admire him.*

Although every woman has not had quite the same experiences that we have had in sharing directly in their husbands' lives—all our circumstances being different—every woman has an opportunity to foster and cement the bonds of her marriage, because all marriages are equally important and valuable to society. And we women know this—will always know this. In this knowledge we are joined once again as women in our ever-changing world.

In a word, we both care, we think we're aware, and we believe that to share is yet another unique gift we women all have.

May everything *you* still know be sounded loud and clear, and may we women realize we owe each other an immense loyalty.

# Two

# To See Ourselves as Others See Us

Oh wad some power the giftie gie us
To see oursel's as ithers see us!
                    —Robert Burns

Women talk all the time.
Women are emotional.
Women are criers.
Women are clinging.
Women don't think logically.
Women love to suffer.

How many times have we heard all these things said about women? And how many times have we started to protest: "You can't talk about women that way, we're not like that at all," and then stopped ourselves? "Well, yes, I know some women like that. Yes, women do cry more than men, and they do like to talk, but so do men. I am more emotional than my husband, and sometimes I make decisions based more on intuition than what he calls logic. And it's not that I cling, but I love my family and want to protect them. Just because I'm able to stand physical discomfort sometimes without a lot of noise, it doesn't mean I enjoy it. . . ."

Every woman is caught up in a dilemma of truth and half-truth about what women are like even when we try to see ourselves as others see us. We hate the stereotypes that say all women are this, all women are that. We dislike it when men say, not joshingly, "Just like a woman." We don't like it when they say, "You women and your constant yakking," when we've been talking about something quite important with a friend. "It's not fair," we think. "Maybe we should get rid of all those stereotypes."

But stereotypes are based on truth; it's not the truth we want to get rid of, only the erroneous feelings people have about them. Perhaps some who fight the stereotypes so avidly are tossing out the baby with the bath water once again and can't see that some of these qualities used productively are very good. Maybe we should reexamine what "women are like" and remind ourselves of what is good about it, what kind of power lies hidden beneath the surface.

In short, what's wrong with sensitivity to emotions, with communicating in the most direct way—by talking? What's wrong with defending your family, with reaching out to others, with enduring trials of mind and body, with acting on what you sense is right rather than on something written down in a logical outline? These are qualities of women that God has granted us, and we should see them as strengths, not weaknesses.

God gave all of us, men and women, a whole

range of emotions—for a purpose. So women seem to shed a briny tear or two more often than men . . . why make such a fuss about it? Women feel deeply and strongly because so much of our life centers on how people relate to us emotionally. And society has given women permission to use tears openly, not to make us "crybabies," but rather to tap the sources of our feelings, to use our sensitivity to human beings for good and kind purposes. We can cry, both in joy or sorrow; we can fully express our emotional and spiritual triumphs and tragedies. We should be grateful this openness of feeling has not been taught to us as a "taboo" as it has been to men.

We know many, many deeply sensitive men, but even most of them don't freely express their emotions the way we do. If only men could learn to show the deep feelings they have, instead of suppressing them under a facade of "manliness." Maybe you've sat beside your husband watching a touching movie or television program. You've been openly touched and teary, and you know well that he's holding back; it's so deeply ingrained that "a strong man doesn't cry." "Big boys don't cry," we say to our sons, and they don't. Ever. If we treasure our own freedom with tears, and know what it represents—a real sensitivity to the emotions within ourselves and what others are feeling—we will want that gift to be shared discreetly by everyone, man or woman.

But what about the other side of the coin, the negative part of that stereotype: that women use their tears selfishly, to get their own way. Every woman knows what she can do with tears. "If I shed a briny tear or two," she thinks, "I'll get my way." We can so easily abuse our ability to express emotion because it seems to provide a simple solution. But few men are so naïve that they don't catch on pretty quickly that a woman is working her wiles and turning on tears to get what she wants. Kids, too, are quick to sense a fake emotion; they're even quicker to ignore it. Oh, it may seem to be working, but each time it's *used* and not truly *felt*, there's something lost: respect, sympathy, a real response . . . and lots of energy!

Yes, women do shed tears sometimes and we can teach our husbands and sons to respect this if we do, and to share in it. But we must also teach our daughters that there is a difference between genuine, spontaneous emotional expression and a cold, calculating "crybaby" use of tears for selfish reasons.

The freedom we have to show how we feel doesn't stop with our tears—they're just one way we have of communicating deeply felt emotions, a symbol of the great gift women have to reveal the invisible world of sensing and feeling that exists side by side with the world of working, eating, sleeping, paying the bills. Think how much is communicated by your hug that tells a child you love him, even though he struck out in the ninth with the bases loaded or how your arms around your daughter reassure her that there is someone who cares, even if the boy of her dreams didn't ask her to the dance. That little kiss in the morning as your husband leaves the house may not be the biggest gesture in the world, but it represents so much. It says, I love you, and I'm the home base you're leaving; and I'll be here when you come back. Millie has a little routine she and Ken go through in the morning when he is leaving for work:

*I always stand at the back door as Ken is leaving for work every morning at 6:45 just to see him off. I always give him the "thumbs up" sign (which in most of the South American countries is a sign that everything is going great!) and he blinks the car lights at me. True, it may seem such a silly little thing to do, but to us it is our last chance to say, again, I love you, before our routine day begins.*

Every woman knows, too, that nothing can communicate like touching, that contact between two people says more than mere words. It says, "I know you're there, I care, and I want you to know I'm here." Those who study childhood development always stress the importance of holding and touching to infants, and they see patterns of delinquency and disordered personalities in children who have largely been deprived of that physical contact from the earliest moments of life. We think the nurturing, holding, touching that women use to express caring isn't something that should be confined to infants; all human beings need it, all through their lives. Women understand its importance. It's not silly, it's not, as little boys have been known to remark, "sissy girl stuff." It's a great, powerful force that creates and strengthens the bonds between people. And interestingly enough, touching in its best sense is *reaching*—and we all need that. We both have experienced the remarkable powers of communicating through touching, just two hands joined or a gesture made without thought but the deepest of meanings.

Millie remembers when holding hands with her future husband once was one of the most exciting things that ever happened to her:

*It was nearly twenty years ago, before Ken and I were married. He started taking me to church with him. I hadn't grown up with the same deep, spiritual background as he had, although I had attended church regularly. But I had always thought of church as a rather strict place where you sat very prim and pro-*

*per.* So one Sunday when I was at church with Ken and he reached over and held my hand, my first reaction was, "This is terrible! You don't do this in church!" But you can, I've learned. It's a marvelous thing, that you can reach out and touch someone you love wherever you are, and it's all right. It's more than all right; it confirms what you have with each other. Even now, after eighteen years of marriage, I like to sit beside Ken in church, with the children on either side of us, so that I can reach over and take his hand in this setting that represents a very important part of our lives.

It's natural to want to reach out to your husband, but we guess even for women it's a little harder to reach out to someone we don't know all that well, yet it's so important both for us and for that other person. Millie has another recollection, about a woman she knew who was going through a real crisis with one of her children:

*I remember one day stopping by the home of a friend and finding her in tears over a situation concerning her daughter. As she told me about the problem, I felt such a tremendous compassion for her that I went over on the spur of the moment and put my arms around her and tried to let her know I knew how much she was hurting and that I cared and wanted to comfort her in some way. I don't think I had ever been that demonstrative with a friend before. Afterward, I felt just a little embarrassed. Later, my friend told me how much that gesture had meant to her. It had lifted her up and made her feel less alone in facing her problem. Today we are closer friends than ever because for one moment I forgot myself and let her know how I felt not by words but by touching.*

26

If we look carefully, we can see how touching our fellow beings opens up a whole new range of spiritual and emotional connections. It's something women seem able to do more easily. Mothering requires it, and that's instinctive, but aren't we a bit less self-conscious than men? Don't we rather naturally want that kind of closeness with other human beings? It's something both men and women need.

Martha's husband, Buckner, is one of those men who understands the important qualities of physical communication. He knows that to communicate, you need your whole self, so he has put things into the services in their very large church that reflect this. Long before books were being written on touching, he had everyone hold hands at some point during the service, hold hands and pray for the person on either side, whatever they needed, whatever their concerns. At the end of the service, always, the worshipers hold hands across the aisles and across the church in one massive experience of touching and communicating. It makes the services very warm and special. One visitor to the church, unfamiliar with the practice, said after the service, "It was like a shock of electricity, that reaching out to hold hands. I really felt as though I *knew* those people on either side of me."

One family, members of the church, had taken a foster child into their home, a teen-age girl who had led an extremely difficult life in the short space of thirteen years. She'd always been deprived of affection and caring that a mother can give, and as she grew older, she became harder and harder to communicate with. Her new foster family wanted so much to help her open up to them and to others and break down the shell she'd built around her, but she remained distant and clearly unhappy.

One Sunday, the family invited her to come

with them to church at Trinity Baptist, and unexpectedly, she agreed to go with them. No one remembered her ever voluntarily or willingly reaching out to touch another person; that was a response she must never have learned. Halfway through the service, Buckner asked everyone to take the hands of the people on either side and join in prayer. The girl hesitated, then took their hands. That experience marked a new beginning for her, or so it seemed to all who knew her. Slowly over the weeks, her foster mother saw her changing as those undeveloped gentle emotional responses were awakened. She came to church each Sunday and joined hands gladly, and we like to think that she was touched, deep inside, by the love flowing from person to person.

No woman should forget in her daily life that her loving hands can make all the difference to another human being. As we and our husbands take the time to hug and hold the children, to comfort and reassure them, and just to affirm to them in a way they can understand that they are loved, it's a real case of actions speaking louder than words, because what we are saying is so vast and so profoundly felt that there really are no words to express it.

Women do love to talk! We do have a "gift of gab." In fact, we two are teased about it often, for we are seldom if ever at a loss for words. It's a way of communicating that all women know. Of course all women know men "gab" too with each other, even when they deny it. But men, we think, do use their ability to talk in different ways. They use it all the time to get from point A to point B in their work, in taking care of their family, in relaxing with friends. Men talk to gain tangible rewards; women talk to make tangible the parts of life that can't be measured or held in the hand. They talk to give shape and reality to qualities of feeling, personality, and motives, and they talk about people's lives because it's a way of comparing their lives with others'. Their talk often has to do with what seems like the little things of life, like raising the children, the home, small events that occur; women are accused then of talking only about trivia. It's small talk, often, but it's talk that's like tiny pieces of a puzzle called "keeping life going successfully." In other words, it's small talk about big things really. This gift of gab we have is really a valuable gift, for it's not just hard facts we seek to convey and understand, but the feelings behind them—the story behind the story.

Nevertheless, we all know that if you talk a lot, you're bound to say something now and then that you shouldn't. The women who make a habit of it sell out their gift of gab to that thing called gossip. And nothing can do quite the harm that gossip can. When a woman uses this means to destroy one's name or reputation, she's in deeper trouble than she could know, for God Himself condemns such action over and over in His Word. When a rumor is started by gossip, it's like taking a big feather pillow and ripping it open in front of a powerful fan. The feathers go all over the place, and it's impossible to go out and collect them again.

Another thing we too often forget is this: We women may be good at talking, but there are two halves to that. One half has to listen, really *must*, and sometimes it's better to remain silent and to try to hear more than the other person is saying. In her anguish and grief, she may be speaking out to you to make some sense out of what has happened to her life. Our finest service may be simply as listener. A woman as listener is one of our greatest unrecognized gifts—if we know when to keep that silence. It's also something that turns up so often in family life. Women are well attuned to listening to their children, but they often forget that their husband especially needs their ear. Listening is one of the really important contributions that a woman can make to her marriage, that sensitive kind of listening her husband can't really get from anyone else. Who would your husband talk to at the office about a situation involving his employees? In a problem with his boss, who can he express his anger or frustration to? He needs the ear only a wife can supply, the listening of the one person who is *always* on his side. Even a working woman, or one with many activities, who has housekeepers and babysitters, who doesn't spend her whole life at home, is still that one person, the one who *wants* to listen. No one else quite shares that special love and partnership that says, "What affects you affects me."

If in nothing else, women everywhere share the knowledge of what it means to endure—that too is a gift. There is a special bond between us. We recognize our need to be steadfast. We women see and understand beyond the boundaries of race, religion, nationality to the common ground we share as females. It comes from biology, the experiences of womanhood, the concerns for home and family that cross frontiers of class, economics, and countries. We are women together, whatever our politics, our jobs, our marital status. Women the world over know what it is to be in love, to be a wife, often to lose a loved one. Mothers know without any language in common what all mothers know and feel. We know about growing up, growing older, about putting aside personal desires for the sake of a greater good. These are the things that define us, and they are all positive, good things. If we fail along our long walks (and no one is human who doesn't stumble now and then), in our hearts we know it. If we succeed, there is, somewhere, another woman who understands what we feel.

That other woman, those millions of women, aren't necessarily the ones we play bridge with, the ones who live next door, the ones who share the school car pool with us. The bonds and the gifts we share are recognized wherever we go.

Millie remembers the Russian woman who sat stolidly night after night in the hall of the hotel in Leningrad where she and Ken were staying for a conference. From early morning until late at night, the woman was always there, stern and unsmiling, watching the well-dressed, affluent visitors from abroad coming and going. She wasn't cute or lovable or quaint and she never spoke. She was just a woman doing a boring job—sturdy, with short, straight hair and plain, shapeless clothes. Yet Millie thought she was admirable somehow, and there was almost nothing she could do to show how much she admired her for sitting there day after day.

*I had a little bottle of perfume that I'd brought with me, and when we were leaving to come home, I took the perfume from my handbag, opened it, and ran it under her nose. Then I handed it to her with a smile that I hoped said everything I couldn't with my three words of Russian.*

*. .At first, she looked at me blankly and then at the little perfume bottle. Then her eyes widened and she smiled, the first smile to appear on her face while we'd been there. Then she reached out and hugged me, and kept saying, "Thank you, thank you" in Russian. I had wanted so much to communicate with her, to say, "Yes, I'm American, I have prettier clothes and more luxuries, but I understand. You care about the same things I do, about being a woman."*

And Martha remembers Maria.

*In 1970, Buckner, our children, and I went to Eastern Europe with a group of young people, a wonderful bunch of singers, on a tour of various churches. In Prague, we were given Maria, our government appointed guide, who traveled through Czechoslovakia and Hungary with us. Our mission of faith was a touchy subject in this whole area, where officially people are free to worship, but not equally free to practice their religion beyond the four walls of the church. Buckner was limited in what he could say—he could bring greetings from San Antonio, and he could fashion a lengthy talk that included Scripture and comments, but someone was always listening. There were no limits, on the other hand, to what the teen-agers and I sang; music is considered culture; sermons might be considered subversive.*

*Maria was in her late fifties, perhaps older. Her English was fair, sufficient to get us all moving in the right direction, for explaining the places we saw, indicating what was permitted and what was not. It was not sufficient for idle chatter, I think, even if Maria had been so inclined, which she was not. She was distant, but not cold. She was kind to us and the children. We began to suspect that she was independent in her way and a freedom lover. She had no patience with "the system" where things didn't work because no one had a real incentive to make them work. I won't forget the sight of Maria with her hair in a sensible bun and her drab, thick coat commandeering taxis in the street to take us to a cultural festival when (to her horror) the buses failed to arrive.*

*One night, when a tram failed to run, Maria led the whole group of us through the streets to catch another. We always sang as we rode or walked, often what the Czechs called the "Glory, Glory Hallelujah" song—"The Battle Hymn of the Republic." (The Russian takeover of 1968 was still fresh in their minds; there were more freedom lovers in Czechoslovakia than just Maria!) Our little singing parade made its way to King Wenceslaus Square, which was still guarded by the armed Russian soldiers who had driven tanks into the city only two years before. I have a photograph taken that night with the soldiers, my family, the teen-agers, Maria, and three or four hundred Czechs who began to gather as we sang, "His truth goes marching on. . . ."*

*. . We had no hint from Maria of what she had lived through in her country all those years, wars, invasions, oppression. There was no hint of a faith that might have sustained her, yet she was with us at all our church services wherever we went in Czechoslovakia, although it was not required of her.*

*. . Our group moved on to Hungary, to Budapest, a city of dreams under a terrible pall, and Maria was assigned to come with us. It was there, in a packed church, that I had one of the most moving spiritual experiences of our trip. I sang a favorite hymn of ours after Buckner had brought greetings:*

> In loving kindness Jesus came
> My soul in mercy to reclaim
> And from the depths of sin and shame
> Through grace, He lifted me.

*As I sang the beautiful description of what happens to a person when he accepts Christ, I looked around the church. The people in front of me were singing quietly with me. It hadn't occurred to me that the Hungarians would know the hymn.*

> He sought me long before I heard
> Before my sinful heart was stirred,

But when I took him at his word,
Forgiven, He lifted me.

*Six-year-old Lisa was sitting down in front beside
Maria as she often did when Buckner and the teen-
agers and I participated in the services.*

Now on a higher plain I dwell
And with my soul I know 'tis well
Yet how or why, I cannot tell
He should have lifted me.

*Everyone in the church was singing now, in Hungar-
ian. As I began the last verse, their voices grew
stronger and louder. It was so moving and wonderful
that I began to cry.*

From sinking sand He lifted me,
With tender hand He lifted me,
From shades of night to plains of light
O praise His name, He lifted me.

*We all sang, and we all cried. There were tears in
Maria's eyes as in everyone else's.*

. . *Then we left Budapest for Vienna, our last
stop. Maria accompanied us only to the spot on the
plain between the two cities, between the free world
and the unfree, where money is exchanged and those
who can leave behind grimness and oppression and,
often, their native land. While Buckner and the boys
were making final arrangements, Maria took me aside.
She spoke shyly of the experience in the church in Budapest; it had touched her in her spirit as it had me.
Slowly she explained how through the years she had
led two lives. She had a spiritual life that no number
of invasions and no political system had been able to
kill. She had a life in the world where she did her job
as a government employee. I was deeply touched by*

34

*her words and by her hidden faith, which to me explained the qualities of persistence and dignity she'd always shown us.*

*Then she said, "I had a little girl. She was like your Lisa. I love your Lisa. My little girl died long ago when she was her age."*

*. . Maria reached into her large purse and handed me a bundle of cloth, bright with many-colored embroidery.*

*. . "When my daughter was ill and dying, the women of my village made this blouse for her. She was never able to wear it. I want your Lisa to have it."*

*Then Maria turned her back on the road to Vienna that we would take and went to the bus that would take her back to her life in Prague. I held in my hands the delicately embroidered blouse that had been meant for a little girl who had died, and I felt that I knew Maria better than I knew a lot of people I see every day. She had shared herself with me in a few words and a gift that was a symbol of our bonds of womanhood and our common spiritual framework. Nothing expresses so well what we all share as women as that gift, motherhood, sorrow, survival, understanding.*

That special gift of understanding is one we should cherish as women, for it makes us grow together instead of dividing us into factions. Our sensitivity to our problems and joys can only sharpen our sensitivity to our husbands, our children, all the people we deal with day in and day out. This is what that gift of feeling means: It isn't weakness but the mark of a strong, sensitive, understanding woman who sees beyond the surface into another's heart.

# Three

# What Makes
# _Your_ World Go Round?

If we have a framework of moral and spiritual values, if we are secure in knowing the range of our inner strength and gifts as women, and if we know that the life-style we've chosen is the right one for us, why is it that some women today still feel uneasy? Today, women are caught in a dilemma. How do we put all the special gifts we have together into a perfect whole, into a way of life that satisfies us and allows us to fulfill God's plan for us and still meet all our responsibilities to others? No wonder these are uneasy and uncertain times. The traditional focus of women's lives has been changing—or has it? When women decide that they're content in homemaking roles, there are still so many voices from every side suggesting that perhaps they're kidding themselves . . . and women ponder these things.

As we've said, women have always known that they look at things differently from men. The world we see and act in isn't precisely the same—and isn't supposed to be. Yet now, strange forces try to make women deny this. So much written about women today separates our lives into pieces and analyzes them over and over. There are hundreds of books on marriage and living complete with pat answers and more analyses. Friends talk with friends and find they have similar pressures. Some husbands don't always understand just what the problem is . . . what women are going through. Even women have that problem sometimes. Sensitive husbands, however, sense a good deal about it. In short, this is a perplexing time for many.

Instead of taking things apart, let's try to put them back together. We're holding a bunch of different spokes and we want to make a wheel. Women have so many fine qualities and abilities, gifts abounding, but they aren't moving us anywhere. We need a hub that we can fix the spokes around. We need a center that holds them all together. We've got to decide on that center, stick with it, and let it make our world go 'round!

Women are lucky. We have a center, even several centers, that are just made to hold those spokes firmly. Once we recognize the hub of our lives, we can adapt to any condition of life, for if the hub is strong, it can hold everything in place. Our identity comes from deep within us—knowing how our lives are centered. It doesn't have to come from jobs we hold in the outside world, or the opinions of others, or how much money we make, how much power we wield, or even what the "in" crowd seems to be doing. It comes from our unswerving knowledge that the identity we've chosen is right for us.

There is the prime center that's available to us

all, men and women. The Lord is there, whether we live in the midst of a family with husband and children or whether we're alone in the world. He will give direction and a shape to any life that desires Him to. His gentleness, innovativeness, and love hold all the major spokes together for anyone who seeks Him. Whatever our condition in life, we can make God our spiritual hub, and know that He will never fail us. "For all those who know your mercy, Lord, will count on you for help, for you have never yet forsaken those who trust in You" *(Psalms 9:10)*. When we must make hard decisions, we can make them knowing that the Lord is there to show the way. When a woman encounters problems in her marriage or in raising children or in other areas of her life, she can comfortably turn to the Lord and pray for His guidance. So often an answer comes, and although nothing external seems to have changed, everything is different. The spokes are oiled and your world is running smoothly and peacefully again. God looks into the heart and knows all the qualities and strengths there. We women know the reality of unseen things, we know our prayers aren't empty words but real communication with that Source of wisdom and strength greater than ourselves—greater than our world or the world's pressures, for Jesus said, "Follow Me . . . I have overcome the world!"

For the Christian, having the Lord as the hub for all the activities of this world is a comfort and a joy . . . and a grand adventure. But our lives are lived out in the bustle of home and family, marriage and jobs, all those people pulling this way and that for our love and attention. We also have pressures and politics and economics and all kinds of aspirations taking us off in a hundred different directions. Women today have so many possibilities available to them;

these should add to our contentment, but sometimes, for some, they don't. How wonderful it is to be able to use the talents God has given us, but instead of knowing where we're going, we often don't know where to turn.

Is it because in this rush toward new goals and activities and equality some women have lost sight of their centers, or have never really secured them, and are drifting, like ships cut loose from their anchors? Women have always needed a personal focus to their lives, and just because our handful of spokes is larger than ever, we still need it—more than ever.

Most women, today as yesterday, still find their real center in their marriage, in lives that revolve around a home and family, whatever else they choose to do. More women than ever today do choose not to marry and they establish a firm focus in their professions; they're still the exceptions. We do believe, however, that the majority of us are most satisfied when we give and get comfort, security, and closeness in the midst of a family, where we can express all those qualities of womanhood that are so natural to us. The intangible realities we feel, we want to make real to our loved ones, our husbands and children.

We want to make real something every woman understands, that something we call "love." Ask any woman why she is married to the man she is, and she'll probably tell you it's because she loves him. But ask her just what she means, and the answer's not so easy—"Oh, you know what I mean. . . ." Of course we do. Every woman knows what it means to love someone. But it's hard to find a simple definition. Is it what books and magazines call love? Romantic escapades we see on television? The grand passions movies show us? Is it really what makes the world go around? It certainly is the secret power that turns the wheel, even though the idea has been cheapened by the media. Love defines us, and our lives.

The following description of love has *never* been equaled. You've heard it and read it so often, but read it now as though for the first time and see how current and dynamic it is: "Though I speak with the tongues of men and of angels, and have not love, I am become as sounding brass or a clanging cymbal. If I have all faith so as to remove mountains, but have not love, I am nothing. And though I bestow all my goods to feed the poor, and though I give my body to be burned, and have not love, it profiteth me nothing."

You may wash and dry millions of dishes, pay all those bills, scrub the floor many thousands of times, make nine million beds, say no a million times to your children. You may endure sickness and sadness, there will be misunderstandings with your husband, there will be crises with the children, times when the bank account is low, times when you will have to give up things, make concessions, sacrifice your dearest dreams. It will all be as dull as it sounds, *unless it is done and saturated with love*. The marriage vows join "better and worse" with "richer and poorer" for good reason. Love in a marriage means doing a lot of things you wouldn't do otherwise. In fact, love is not even thinking about the doing of them at all—it somehow propels you in a strange way. Love is a bright coat of paint that makes those less-than-fun things bearable, just as it is the warm, glowing candle that lights up our places of joy. Love defines the center that holds our spokes together better than we can define love.

"Love is very patient and kind, never jealous or envious, never boastful or proud. Never haughty or selfish or rude. Love does not demand its own way. It is not irritable or touchy. It does not hold grudges and will hardly even notice when others do it wrong. It is never glad about injustice, but rejoices whenever truth wins out. If you love someone you will be loyal to him no matter what the cost. You will always believe in him, always expect the best of him, and always stand your ground in defending him. All the special gifts and powers from God will someday come to an end, but love goes on forever . . . Love never fails. . . ."

Love is an active verb. It is always doing, showing, helping, feeling, sharing, taking as well as giving. Love is never still. It is unchanging in its greatest definition, yet growing, expanding to encompass the whole center of our lives, surrounding us with caring and being cared for. And all these words that go into defining love are the words we use to describe what women at their best do, what we are. This is certainly not something we should think of as a liability, but something the world needs desperately. Love . . . makes the world go 'round!

How true it is of us women that we can recognize so much of our identity in and through what we love. Now that sounds, on the surface, as though we're suggesting that a woman surrender her identity as an individual in her marriage. We're not. We're simply saying love has a way of satisfying a woman's needs—and it's a recognized treasure to women—our hearts are happy and satisfied when we're in love. That's not a new concept. Jesus said, "Where your treasure is, there shall your heart be also." One follows the other.

The oneness in marriage that is worked out through love doesn't come easily. It's not a simple task for a woman to fix a handful of spokes around the hub she has chosen and make it work. It doesn't just happen when the preacher says, "I now pronounce you husband and wife." The love that works itself out in people's lives has to have time to grow. Sadly, in many marriages, it doesn't ever happen ever. In others, it takes a long, long time because both man and woman are growing up as their love grows up. Often, we've seen it happen through a crisis in a couple's life: a serious illness, a misunderstanding cleared up, something that makes them aware of what they mean to each other, what they have going for them. The love that has been invested in the early, happy days of a marriage is transformed and, more important, is transforming into a deeper relationship than ever could have been at the beginning.

"My husband isn't perfect," a woman will say, "but I love him, so I'll change him." Maybe he has a hang-up about money, or he isn't a romantic man who buys flowers. He repeats his favorite stories too often, he never hangs up his clothes. He isn't this, he doesn't do that. And I'm going to change him.

Well, that's a real misunderstanding of the power of our love to change a person. Love's power to transform isn't selfish or petty. A lot of the changes a woman wants to make "because she loves him" aren't for her husband's sake at all. They're for her own sake, picking out so-called flaws instead of concentrating on the good qualities—and the fact that she loves her husband . . . and has the really important things going right.

The love we're talking about isn't selfish, nor is it a conditional love that asks for something in return. That's the way God loves us. It's the kind of love that brings a genuine response in the human heart. It's the love that transforms a crisis in marriage into a stronger, better relationship. Every Christian seeks to follow the perfect model for unconditional love that we've been given in Jesus Christ. Every human being will find that this kind of love can't be resisted when it goes into action.

"Jesus said, 'I will never leave you or forsake you.' That's all I had to hang on to in that awful time a few years back when I saw myself being forsaken by my husband." The young woman who said this is a mutual friend of ours who shared her story with us. We saw her move from what seemed to be a conventionally happy marriage into a time of real crisis where the center of her life started to slip away. And we saw her regain what she had had and more because she went back to the true hubs of her life, her faith in God and her total love for her husband.

"I always thought of my husband as the best, and I never felt that I deserved him. Deep down inside, I had the feeling that it couldn't last, that what I had was going to be taken away, no matter how much I loved him. Well, it almost happened. How almost isn't important anymore, how he gradually became involved with another woman and I could see it happening. It was like a bad dream come true. The more my anguish showed, the farther away it drove him. When he came home, he heard nothing good—the usual problems with our several children plus my terrible mental state because I could see what was happening to us. It just got worse and worse, and I didn't know what to do. I used to think that the fact that I loved him so much meant that I could hold him, but it wasn't enough. My love was totally selfish, it came out of that fear of losing him that was there right from the beginning.

"I believe now with all my heart that God lets these things occur in your life to temper you, the way fine gold is tempered. It strips away your complacency and your fear and really tests your love, proves its strength. I'm not saying that unless you've suffered and almost gotten a divorce you're not going to have a marvelous relationship with your husband. But sometimes you have to be shown what is real and what is not real. Some women have to have their little world shaken up to find out what really means something to them.

"I found that what was real was my husband and my family. I started with just that. I had nothing or no one to fall back on but the Lord and the knowledge that I didn't want to lose my husband. It wasn't easy to live through that time. I kept saying, 'Lord, why? Don't you want families to stay together?' I couldn't bring myself to say, 'Lord, if it's your will for me and my husband to get a divorce, I can accept that.' All I thought I wanted was what *I thought was best for me*. It took a long while to be able to say, 'Lord I know *you* want the best for me. Help me say, "Whatever road I have to take to get that best, I'm willing to do it." ' When I could truly say that and mean it, my anxiety and fear fell away. He did give me the best. He worked on me and He worked on my husband, and now we have a relationship that didn't begin to exist until we passed through that terrible time.

"I know that what I faced a lot of women face. I hope they can know that it isn't necessarily the end of their life because they're having a struggle in their marriage. I know that a lot of our problems came from fear, the fear that I was inadequate, undeserving, and that great fear so many of us have, that we'll be left . . . alone. I loved my husband for what I got back from him for me. Then I learned, in desperation, that loving him, period, was all that I could do. It was a gift of God, and He held my marriage together, because it was within His will . . . and I've never felt

45

more aware of who I am and how valuable I am to this relationship and this world. I have a great deal to give!"

One of our *very* favorite Scriptures is God's promise that all things work together for good to them that love the Lord—to them that are called according to His purpose—to them who've made Him the hub of their life.

No, this kind of love doesn't make us spineless creatures at all. Our talent for love of this sort is one of the things that make us different—and essential. For it's the difference between the sexes, the complementary nature of men and women, the different qualities and sensitivities that each brings to a marriage that makes it work. One of Martha's friends, Ruth Graham, says that if she and her husband, Billy, always agreed on everything, one of them would be unnecessary. If men and women were identical in their thoughts and feelings, way of looking at the world or accomplishing tasks, and in their contributions to a marriage, marriage itself would be unnecessary. Marriage isn't a contest, it shouldn't be a battleground, but it should be two parts that work together, making up for a lack here, contributing wisdom or a quality there, receiving different impressions of a situation and sharing them to reach a conclusion. A man may see a situation in terms of politics or power, money, approval from the outside world; a woman, in terms of meaningful values, emotions, security, the interaction of human beings. Who can say that a man's way is bold and adventurous, a woman's not? There's no greater adventure, really, than a woman setting out on marriage and motherhood; this is surely equal to any man's adventure into unknown lands or an ambitious climb to power and importance.

That's true equality, when every man and every

woman has the freedom to do and be what each is capable of. We women, as much as men, have failed to recognize the real value of the qualities of womanhood we bring to the world and especially our marriages. Yet they show in so many ways.

"I hope I don't die before my husband," a woman told Martha many years ago, "because there are some things I know that he doesn't." It takes a good number of years to understand fully what she was talking about. At the time, she said, "Take the children. I know things about the children that he doesn't. Tommy has to be tucked in a certain way, he likes you to rub his back. Jimmy doesn't like his back rubbed. Susan always wants you to kneel down and pray with her before bed, but the other two like to say their prayers alone. Their father is a wonderful, loving father, but he just doesn't know . . . hasn't had the time and opportunity to."

We read a delightful story somewhere about a woman who always has to call home to remind her husband to take the trash out. "Surely it doesn't take the two of you to do that," a friend said.

"Well, it does actually," she replied. "I can't manage the garbage cans, and he can't manage to remember. But together we can do it."

*. .Together we can do it* is a magic, motivating element in marriage. Too often some women can't seem to feel its importance and some men hardly think about it at all—but it's powerful. Women extremists at both ends of the spectrum have trouble with this because one group wants to be totally independent of anyone while the other wants total dependence. We just can't identify with either of these extremes, for we've experienced the powerful partnership that marriage means, and we feel that most women think this way too. They see the reality and

strength of that statement—*together we can do it*—and they know that their real and important job is being a partner in marriage. This partnership is the most dynamic and influential of all human partnerships. For the lives they touch, the innocent children they nurture, and the homes they build either bless or blight the very foundations of our society. No small partnership here. Not on your life.

One of the challenges of being a partner in marriage is in deciding priorities in how that marriage is going to be arranged to make it work. Every marriage is different, but in most cases the man is and will continue to be the major breadwinner. That is all tied up with our survival and means that for most women who've chosen this role, the big responsibility is making it possible for him to go out there to work. She's the one who makes sure he's fed and clothed, comforted, renewed; she cares for the home; she makes it possible for the children to go out and learn what they must know to survive. And out of necessity, she's the one who has that ticklish job of deciding on many of the priorities. She endeavors to see how the family is going to work it all out, how every single one of the family members gets to be heard, and she constantly reviews her hats set out all in a row and decides which one she's going to wear . . . when . . . and where . . . that day. If she has a firm grasp on the mechanics of making the lives of all those she's responsible for work she couldn't possibly feel that she has an insignificant job. It takes enormous brainpower and organization. Her husband is the hub in terms of society and the home. He is the head of the house. Not a tyrant; not the *only* maker of decisions; but the head . . . *by her choice.*

Sometimes we have to surrender something, in life, in marriage, to reach a greater goal. It is not one-sided, both men and women do this, but we're talking about women right now. "Is it fair?" women ask. "Why should I give up something so that my husband can do something else?" Sometimes we have to surrender the privilege of "being in charge." And that's awfully hard if we're born with strong personalities and a real liking for taking command. But this is really not as sacrificial as it might appear. In a good partnership, it really works, whatever the personalities of the couple. There's room—lots of it—for everybody's opinions and even decisions, for decisions seem to be ceaseless and countless in the day-in-ness and the day-out-ness of marriage, children, and the home. Sometimes—many times—a woman knows she should go ahead and decide this or that, knowing her husband well enough to know he'd like a break now and then. There's a healthy balance in a good marriage, and neither the husband nor wife wants everything left to him or her. We've never met any "critter" like that in a *good* marriage—the balance works rather automatically really.

There are plenty of marriages where strong, practical, realistic women are married to impractical dreamers; where lively, extroverted women have quiet, unassuming husbands. Yet they are good and happy marriages. "Cool it, honey," a husband may say and his wife will know that she has reached a limit in her "take-charge-ism." If she trusts his judgment and knowledge of her, she knows that sometimes he knows better than she what her limits are, just as she knows his. "What do you think we ought to do about this situation?" asks the practical woman who thinks she knows perfectly well what should be done (and may even have said so). Unless her husband has surrendered all decision making, he has his chance, as head of the family, to decide what's to be done. The strength of a marriage lies in a genuine partnership, where each contributes strengths and qualities, and each knows when to stop and listen.

We had the opportunity a few years ago to meet an exceptional woman, whose claim to fame was that she was married for more than fifty years to an internationally famous preacher. We knew him, certainly; in his later years, he was almost a living legend in church circles, a man who could preach the stars down, a dynamic man who made his mark on everyone who heard him. Until we met the sweet, grayhaired lady who was his wife, we'd never heard of her much at all.

"What a great man you're married to," someone said to her politely while almost everyone gathered around her husband.

"I see what a great man I've made," she said with a twinkle in her eye and the trace of a smile. And then everyone listened to her, especially all the women married to important, dynamic men.

"It wasn't always easy to make it clear to him what I knew to be right and wrong, and even a preacher can go off on the wrong track. It wasn't easy to keep from being almost overwhelmed by a man like that. I understood *his* greatness and strongly felt *I* had something to contribute, too.

"I'll never forget our first church, oh, many, many years ago. A little country church, very conservative. I was a very young wife, and I hadn't had a lot of experience being married to a pastor. I remember I had a new red velvet evening dress I thought was wonderful, and I couldn't wait for a chance to wear it. The ladies of the church had a tea to welcome me, the new pastor's wife, and of course I wore my dress. The ladies promptly formed a committee to tell me that it was not an appropriate dress for the pastor's wife. I think my husband silently agreed with them, but nevertheless, after I thanked them for coming, I made plans to wear the dress again every chance I got. I was going to wear it until they understood that this was what I was like; I liked red velvet dresses. I wore it to everything I possibly could until they understood that I was me and that was all there was to it.

"I remember another time one Sunday morning when my husband got it into his head that he would preach against wearing fingernail polish. Maybe he thought it was too worldly for the women of the church, but I thought it was not a very important sermon topic. It seemed to me that there were plenty of things that had priority over nail polish; I knew he was getting off the track, and it was up to me to make it clear to him. So that Sunday afternoon, I made sure, before the evening service, that I had freshly done, glistening red fingernails when I went to church.

" 'Didn't you hear your husband?' one of the ladies whispered to me.

" 'Yes,' I said. 'But someone has to suggest that he has no business preaching on something so trivial. There are greater verities in life than the wearing of nail polish, and the person to tell him is his wife. I love him too much to see this happen. He is a remarkably great man—one of the greatest—too great for this.'

"I made my point, that nail polish was beyond the limit. I knew, and he did, too, that if he allowed himself to go too far out of line, he could have gotten onto some really peculiar subjects, even farther away from what his real business was. And you know something, he respected me and was wonderful about what I did—he loved a love like that!"

We laughed and laughed and so loved this lady in every way along with her husband—and Martha tossed a special bouquet of praise for her own preacher husband, Buckner, who "so beautifully majors on the majors" and even loves her nail polish.

How much more effective than tears or turmoil, that wonderful special power of women to make our judgments and opinions clear in ways other than words. We have looks and actions, the red fingernails that speak pages. We're lucky that this is one of the ways we see the world—not as something that can only be put into words but a whole range of expressions on a whole range of subjects, symbols instead of sound waves. Any woman who thinks about it realizes that there are so many occasions when this way of making things clear is put to use; it's almost an instinctive way we have of communicating.

It's a wonderfully effective language—but only if between wife and husband there is a real oneness that makes the translation possible. The man who says truthfully, "I just don't understand women" is probably talking about our symbolic language that he's not tuned into, and he's probably unmarried or his marriage isn't a good and close one. In good marriages, in fact, lots of the deepest communication is just that way, for ideas are being expressed that are not only difficult but impossible to put into words. Very often, we are expressing the love that makes our world go 'round.

We can go back again to the Bible, to Paul who was able to say so well in words what we find difficult to express. We are bond slaves to the Lord, he said; not persons bought into slavery but persons who *choose* to serve. He said, "It is not anything I'm forced to do that makes me serve Christ. It is the love of Christ that constrains me. *His love for me makes me want to serve Him.*"

This is the mutual joy that we seek in our marriages and the way we women want love to work. There is marvelous joy in seeing your husband as the head of the house, the center of your life—and how especially so when you've got a head of the house who thinks *you're* fantastic!

# Four

# Under Her Nose—
# And She Blew It!

So we've decided what makes our world go 'round and we believe we have our centers straight—what about the men today? If ever they were saying, "I don't understand women," it should be today! Women are even having a problem understanding themselves. They have an uneasy feeling that there's an "enemy" in their land and, as one writer states: "The enemy, they realize at first uneasily and then with growing hostility, is primarily other women." This is confusing to everyone—how can this happen? And are there not two extremes? Aren't most women somewhere between?

Men are bound to be confused if they read half of the material written about women or even hear half of what's being said. Husbands go from at least wondering to total perplexity if they think about it at all.

And they're thinking about it all right. We read the other day about a man describing his wife's entrance into the business world: "She felt she needed to go into the 'real world.'" What "real" world? Ask people who are in the business world—we've both been there—you'll find just as much phoniness there as anywhere else.

The man said his wife felt she "needed" to go into the *real* world. Why? Who made her feel this way? If it was her own honest desire to extend her talent, or if she had no other choice because of financial need, or if it was *her* decision—fine. But if it was media pressure on her, propaganda that makes her think she just isn't "with it" unless she leaves home, then who's to blame?

Surely the pressure is on; voices on every side try to shout their propaganda into the world's ear and make us think they're speaking for all women. No way. But, let it be said here that, though it's difficult even to think sometimes in this noisy atmosphere, it's desperately necessary that we do, or we lose our ability to know what we really want and to hear the voice of our own conscience. This voice is very difficult to hear sometimes in the midst of all the other voices— loud, electronic, and very persuasive. We must always remember this and we need God's help to do so. But, if we, with integrity and resolve, respond to our *own* feelings and needs thoughtfully and sincerely, then we are truly liberated even from the most clamorous voices. And we are able to act confidently upon what we *know* to be right for us.

So, if this wife, out of *her* need and desire, made her own decision with honesty and understanding, she, in all probability, remained well aware where the real and valued world is. But, let us say here, the home-loving woman who cops out and fails to be strong in the face of all those who would tell her her life is wasted if she has not moved beyond her home, will never accomplish much at home or beyond it.

The point is being aware of what's real and unreal—and being aware here is vital to real liberation!

We were sharing some of these thoughts with a close friend, a mother of several girls, and she responded very quickly with a note of distress in her voice: "My girls think they are not doing right just being at home—that they should be somewhere else, too, for reasons they can't really come up with." Now, all these girls are young mothers, but they seemingly don't see the challenge. Why? Is it not there or is it that many women have watched only the onslaught of the sexual revolution and the women's liberation movement and have failed to see the coinciding increased divorce rate and breakdown of family values—and have themselves become victims?

Where is the real world? It's where real people are. At HOME! If you can't be real at home, you're in trouble and so is home. Robert Frost's great insight here touches us:

Home is the place where,
     When you have to go there
They have to take you in.

I should have called it
Something you somehow
     Haven't to deserve.

You can be real in a place "you haven't to deserve," for all your best efforts are voluntary. It's at this point that we see why home is so essential. Outside of the church (when it is being its noblest best), where can you go that you can be you? Only one place: home!

Even heaven is called home, as are all situations where we are esteemed for being who we are: "Make yourself at home!" "This is like home to me!" "There's no place like home!" "Home is where the heart is!"

It's a powerful place! Lots goes on here! Lives are in the making here! Worlds are changed here, as Konrad Adenauer so aptly reminded us: "When the world seems large and complex, we need to remember that great world ideals all begin in some home neighborhood." The "real" world out *there*—foolishness! It's *here*—under our noses!

Homemaking has taken a bum rap during the last decade. It is considered by society as "square," obsolete, dull; all right only if you can't do anything else worthwhile; it's old-fashioned and really not very worthy of esteem. The real world of the home has been made to look like a rather quaint, shallow place where you might pop in and out, but where certainly not much happens. Rather than a strong resort, it's pictured as the "last" one. Absurd. More goes on here than the mind can comprehend, but it's pictured today so often as the place full of detergents and furniture polishes and floor waxes rather than a house full of hearts and feelings and needs. Do we let this happen to relieve us of our responsibilities? Isn't it easier to polish a floor than an ego? To mend a seam than a broken heart? To restore furniture rather than relationships? Oh, we'd better see what goes on here—maybe we'd better go home and take a look.

Just *staying* at home, however, doesn't guarantee doing well at homemaking either. Whether you're at home all the time or part of the time, it's your realization of its remarkable importance, your giving your best to it, that colors all you and your family do and all that you are. It must be one of our cherished treasures, for Jesus said: "Where your treasure is, there will your heart be also."

One of our friends, who for financial reasons has to work, was speaking of her uneasiness about this, for she is home-oriented, a devout homemaker, and worries if her small quantity of time there has real quality. However, she was reassured the other day, when her ten-year-old son said, "Wow, mother, you teach school, you teach Sunday school, and you teach us!" Now she has it all together because she knows where the values lie. As we've said, women can deal with priorities if they recognize them.

Like the perfectly delicious cake that rises to heights of beauty and taste, lots of ingredients go into making a house a home, and also making a woman rise to her highest and best as a superb homemaker. Naturally, she herself needs to see the challenge. She most often does at the beginning, and then wrong ingredients can come in to sour it all.

One of these is an atmosphere in the home of "taking her for granted." A husband can, by his warm sensitivity and thoughtfulness, keep a woman going strong, happy, and creative, or he can knowingly or unknowingly give off "boss-like" demands and very little warmth about her role. The children often catch his spirit. She then feels used—and who wouldn't? She rebels and feels no challenge left after enough of this. A smothering person runs for air.

A woman must feel self-esteem in her role, knowing that she's honored for herself and not just what she does in her home. For to her it's not a trade, but a calling; not an occupation, but a dedicated life's work. Ideally, every member of the family, *everyone*, should be honored for being themselves at home, for real love frees one to be himself or herself—while possessive love is enslaving. We have all seen too many home situations where either the husband or wife has confused possessiveness with love and they somehow don't realize they're smothering the other's very identity.

Susan has a tough time trying to figure out her husband's "love":

"I really want to be an ideal wife. I love him so much. I think—or thought—he loved me too, but . . . I don't know, I just don't understand. . . .

"He claims to care for me deeply, but he wants me to always be a little dowdy, just not quite up to par. He said he loves me this way. I know, and he does, that I'm not at my best—I feel down a lot. But he keeps me in line, by assuring me that this is how he loves me . . . not too, oh, I guess, you'd call it well-groomed . . . and he wants me to do pretty much exactly what he commands. Well, I noticed something. . . .

"When we were with friends the other evening, he spent his time complimenting the other women on how they looked. He really liked *them* the way I *want* to be. What *is* happening? I'm beginning to think *he's* insecure. And I'm beginning to think I'm falling *out* of love . . . if we ever had it to start with."

Susan is at present trying very hard to do her part to work through this problem. She's concerned and seeking help. Her husband's eyes may be opening too, but their problem will never be solved until he honors her own personhood and she begins to help him feel secure in his own. For there's great responsibility for each of them—she needs to be strong and courageous, and he needs to see how unreasonable he has been. This is tough, but there is hope. Because the "no nonsense" business of working things like this out is conducted in the "realest" world of all—home.

In the atmosphere of unselfish love, our homes

are nourished and our marriages flourish, for with love like that, marriage is not on any percentage basis other than 100%/100%. And each upholds and confirms the other—no forced allegiance here, but each encouraging the other to be him or herself in a tough world. And a tough world it is. We both believe in being real at home and in fostering this in our families the best we can, for home is the training camp for being real in public life. A counterfeit at home is a counterfeit in the business world—and vice versa. So, for genuineness, we need to start where the starting place is—at home.

Martha enjoys finding meaningful poems and statements and framing them for her husband's desk in his office. She was impressed a long time ago with a statement she found along these very lines:

*One day, I saw this statement on a little card. It was a perfect description of the struggle every human being has, particularly in public life, when it would be so easy to be something you're not in order to please everybody. But in spiritual things, if God is in them, genuineness is no option—it is an essential ingredient. So on my husband's desk is this one of our very favorite statements. It has been there nineteen years:*

> to be nobody—but—yourself—
> in a world which is doing its best,
> night and day,
> to make you everybody else—
> means to fight the hardest battle
> which any human being can fight;
> and never stop fighting.
> —e. e. cummings, Letter 1955

*That's it! Home is the place where we can be ourselves. It should be where we're praised for it!*

We must mention the ingredients that really add the flavor of life at its fullest—children! They're remarkable creatures who keep you with your feet on the ground and your heart turned to heaven. They're the stuff out of which human beings are made, and they make human beings out of their parents—real quick! Hurrah for kids! Every age is challenging and disarming and charming altogether!

Let's change the words of the familiar song to: ". . . when you become a parent/By your children you'll be taught!" They do teach, too, and in those fresh and early years, they work out of an untarnished understanding of what matters the most in living life to the fullest. "Out of the mouths of babes" we do learn if we will listen. We're nurtured too. Then, when the world hits them hard and heavy, we *must* be strong nurturers for these potential world-beaters! They *must* find strength and stability at home in order to be strong and helpful in this challenging world. These little persons and their needs are not casual—not at all—and a woman who *knows*, knows that the elegance of mothering and helping her children is inestimable in value, no second-rate job, for children are the priceless ingredients that make home a potential powerhouse that moves beyond its own sphere—to the world! She knows that when she helps a child, she ". . . helps humanity with an immediateness which no other help given to human creatures in any other stage of human life can possibly give again."

In short, almost every woman still knows that there's no place on earth where she is more innately gifted and equipped to comprehend its meaning than home! She can confidently select that sphere as her *only* career and be assured that there's a majesty about it, or she can make whatever length of time she's able to be at home remarkably productive in quality all the way, for she *knows* she *must not fail here* at any cost! She *knows* that any other of her successes bought at the cost of her home and family are strangely and surely tarnished!

From an Ann Landers column?

Someday the liberated woman will discover that her most important job, the one with the greatest rewards, was right under her nose— and she blew it.

Thank God for the women who haven't!

# *Five*

# *Say That Again?*

When women feel those things that they innately cherish are threatened, they react—wisely at first perhaps, and then often in a puzzling, extreme manner. One of the extremes in the women's world today is that wind we all sense blowing through the land that seems to demand those values most women deeply cherish—marriage, home, and children. And so, in strong reaction to this we get the opposite end of the spectrum, another extreme. Another phenomenon. A revolution. This extreme needs to be seen carefully too—in the bright light of honesty. Truth's spotlight is incredibly bright, totally revealing, and a sure guiding light to the *right* path. We believe every woman really wants to follow this right path—particularly in her marriage, in her home which is so much *her*. So let's take a good, honest look at this other extreme.

65

On the streets of New York, during the earliest fervor of the women's liberation movement a woman was questioned about the movement. She replied with a bit of humor: "I certainly do *not* believe in women's lib. I want to be a *slave* to my husband—I can control him better that way!" We remember reading this and laughing over and over at her candor. A joke, gang, that's what it was! A fun comment on women and their "wiles." Every woman knows she has them and she ought to know how to handle them with care. This was a tongue-in-cheek response of a happy woman who had lots of warm humor and saw the ridiculousness of extremes—surely *not* the basis of a serious life-style. Surely not a serious life-style made to appear as moral! Surely not the life-style of a devoted, thoughtful, and intelligent wife. But unfortunately that philosophy is tricky when not seen for what it is and has even fooled the women using it into thinking they're being unassertive and nondomineering. But we promised to take a good look, didn't we? The serious use of this kind of philosophy—"I will not compete with my husband, so I'll be a 'doormat' for him"—did come about first as a reaction to the most extreme element of the women's liberation movement. Unfortunately, it's turned into the strangest of all situations: The woman *now* is competing by using another of her "gifts"—her wiles—to get her way, still under the guise of self-sacrifice and subservience. Incredible. No wonder men throw up their hands in disbelief—and most women we know do too. We feel so earnestly the need to tell women who have felt defeated at both extremes—either by the lib movement or the "doormat" approach—that there are multitudes of women who have used their fine gift of sensing and who have found satisfaction dealing in *real* relationships rather than manufactured ones. The devastation felt by women who, in desperation, becoming something "fake" to try to build something "real" is overwhelming when they are made to feel that this is their only alternative. Not so! God is the Lord of reality, and "play like" is a children's game—a childish thing that the Bible tells us to put away when we become grown-up. Marriage is not basically a contract, but a relationship, and it takes two people to relate.

Now our deep concern about the consequences of the "doormat" philosophy comes not from brash women's libbers, but from two women who are serious believers in Jesus Christ, who have always felt great liberation because of Him and His real emancipation of women in general and specifically ourselves personally—*personally!* It comes from contented wives who freely do their thing, with the blessing, support, and encouragement of their very strong, secure, and loving husbands—women who likewise love them, encourage them, and really want them to fulfill their dreams. It comes from both of us who have seen so many, many wives whose marriages are in trouble, try this fake submissive approach only to feel even less self-esteem than ever before—and whose husbands can't really figure out what's going on! In a sense, this manufactured approach has figured in avoiding honest relationships rather than in "fortressing" them. We know that often this approach was originally born out of a kind of sincerity we all can understand, for when women feel their marriage slumping they usually do try to do something about it. And often, if they're honest, they see that they've not really kept the sparkle of marriage intact; they've not bolstered their husbands as they know they can and should. They've let themselves go or they've become naggers—oh, all sorts of things.

So all women do need to keep tabs on themselves, to shape up, but *genuinely*, not as a gimmick. (And, by the way, this kind of slump in marriages can be brought on by men too. *Both* men and women have to keep things fresh.) When the noble effort becomes a game of manipulation, that's not good nor healthy. It may be paraded as the "Christian" way—as dogma, as a moral absolute, as the only alternative— but looked upon closely, it is a cleverly disguised form of manipulation of the worst sort, born more out of women's personal desperation than a biblical revelation! We women understand ourselves well enough to know how wily we can be. To lift this to a Christian absolute is unsound and damaging indeed! We know of very few men who would not recognize that they were being "controlled" and very few women who wouldn't own up to the selfishness of their feigned unselfishness. We two are speaking at this point about an honest relationship in marriage because this is vital to women's happiness; we can't "play like" here and be fulfilled.

Our strong impression about the importance of seeing extremes for what they are has grown not out of theory but out of many years of involvement with people. Not casual acquaintances or chance conversations here and there, but out of decades of pilgrimage. We have seen and are seeing many marriages hurt— really hurt—by adhering to either of these extremes in the women's world today. Marriage is delicate and yet can withstand much; however, we need always to be aware of destructive influences from either extreme. Most people we know are not interested in wasting time on cheap imitations of the real thing; they cherish and respect their marriage intensely.

To present as the only alternative to the women's liberation movement a form of behavior that degrades women, maneuvers men, and makes "things" out of both is indeed a sad, sick picture. And sadder than that is to present it as Christian! To equate Christianity with "acting" is the ultimate hypocrisy, for Christ devastated as heretics the "play-actors" or "hypocrites" in all His teaching. Can you begin to imagine what He would say about "playacting" at life's most sacred human relationship—marriage?

We must *not* mix things up—and, oh, how we do in our day. We confuse sex with love, loudness with importance, playacting with reality, license with liberty, activity with accomplishment, noise with courage, power with authority, and selfish manipulation with submission! We baptize our faults and turn our vices into virtues with very clever mental gymnastics. We human beings have always been pretty adept at this individually, but it becomes extremely dangerous when accepted as a life-style for larger and larger groups of people. A whole nation can go down—thinking it's progressing upward!

So how should we look at things and not be deceived? William Blake says it well:

This life's dim windows of the soul
Distorts the heavens from pole to pole
And leads you to believe a lie
When you see *with* not *through* the eye.

[italics added]

What does that mean? We women ought to know—that's our gift—to see things soulfully. We think it takes looking at things with your heart and soul also, most thoughtfully, with God's wisdom and guidance and much prayer to discern. There's no human being with the "smarts" enough to sort it all out. No matter what *anyone* says, we simply can't do it right alone!

We are all vulnerable in this tricky world, and so needy, and Jesus promises to supply our needs.

Resorting to a kind of fake approach is not viable, because as real as needs are in marriage or whatever, so are the answers if faced *squarely*.

A word must be said about the often-quoted portion of Scripture: "Wives, submit yourselves to your husbands. . . ." That's not the whole verse or the whole passage of Scripture, and to quote it as such is damaging and unsound Biblical interpretation to any knowledgeable Bible student. It goes on: "Husbands, love your wives just as Christ loved the church and gave His life for it." But let's not limit its full meaning with even this passage, for it all begins really at the beginning of this wonder-filled mammoth letter to the Christians in Ephesus. Paul is telling them some of the wonderful results that will show in their relationship to others when they *first* submit themselves to the Lord. He is helping them sort it all out; he prays for them, thanks God for them, and he expects great things from them. His entire thesis, inspired by God, from the beginning of the book, is how we as Christians should act and behave toward others in *all* situations, and in particular, and specifically in the fifth chapter, in the area of *marriage*. It's made totally clear that a strong vertical relationship to God comes *first* before human, horizontal relationships.

Why on this needy earth is this "real" basis of Christian marriage in the first place so strangely ignored? It's not fair to the Spirit of Jesus Christ to leave this background out, so we won't. Paul is saying that first of all, before *any* human relating can be done well at all—in marriage or life in general—each person must have that remarkable vertical relationship with God clear and strong and honest. For we can't begin to know ourselves and what kind of folks we are to live with until we let God, who made us, reveal this to us lovingly and strongly. We need that first! Then, maybe we can relate to someone else honestly. Let's go on. It needs to be pointed out that since all human relationships are predicated on mutual submission to the Lord first, all our human relationships are transformed—and specifically the relationships of husbands and wives. If our being able to relate nobly even to a total stranger is dependent on a strong vertical relationship with our Lord, how much *more* would this be important in the close "togetherness" relationship of marriage.

"Can two walk together, except they be agreed?" *(Amos 3:3).*

Basic faith in the Lord is really not a casual option for the happiest, most enriching marriage—that's where the passage earlier quoted really begins. Then there are some words God speaks, through Paul, to both husbands and wives—not just wives alone! OK now, we are hearing: "Wives, submit yourselves to your husbands . . ."—but there is not a period here . . . it goes on: "Wives, submit yourselves to your husbands *as to the Lord.*" Look closely here . . . as to the *Lord*—that *same* Lord Jesus Christ who risked His life and ministry to raise the standard of all women in that day of their greatest bondage! That same Lord who upset all the establishment's, preconceived, enslaving ideas of womanhood! Why, He even threw one village into chaos by saying publicly, in defense of all women who were harshly judged, "Do you see this *woman?*"—her worth, her potential, *herself!* He set her free! In fact, you could read the New Testament over and over and *never* find an instant when Jesus did not set the woman free! Over and over and over again. And He told them over and over to "go in peace!"—*the most majestic description of liberation ever heard.*

Peace! and liberation *inside*—where it must be to really count! ". . . as unto *that* kind of Lord!"

Now isn't it a strange contradiction that in the *very* name of Jesus, the Great Liberator, unenlightened Christians have, through the misuse of one word, reinstated the subservient role of women that He died to abolish. In the name of the Light of the World they have reverted to the darkness of despotism! Incredible.

Do hear this! Out of this mutual submission to the Lord grows this loving relationship between husbands and wives, and the husband is equally spoken to and called upon to give the supreme ultimate kind of love—sacrificial love—when he hears these powerful words: "Husbands, love your wives just as Christ loved the church and gave His life for it." We now have pictured here the spiritual ideal in marriage that frees us in the name of the "Son that makes us free indeed"—frees us to be and give and love each other to the fullest, for when two people are submissive to the Lord and are one, a woman's submission can *never* be interpreted as slavery nor the man's sacrificial love used as dictatorship. Therefore, all husbands and wives must begin at the same point—with the Lord—then marriage is a loving covenant, not a contract.

Do we realize the incredible spiritual strength in all of this, how it works? Here we have described a husband who would die for his wife, married to a woman who is innately *made* to respond in all of her senses to that kind of love—we all are. We women truly do respond to real, thoughtful, warm, gentle, strong, and powerful love from our men. We're created to—no doubt about it! Love like that constrains a woman to respond not calculatingly, but naturally with a love so real that it doesn't even think of itself as submissive or any other term—it's truly fulfilling and complete. Both partners give and receive in harmony that defies technical description. It's what we believe it's all about, ideally. This is not to say there's no work involved—there is—on the part of both partners, both being larger than life because of the other. When the Bible speaks of the two becoming one, that's a miracle; it's mutual, and it really, truly happens. Love between a husband and wife ought to be bigger than measurement, such as: "I'll submit today," "You surrender tomorrow," "I'll give fifty percent, you give fifty percent." Ridiculous! It's as delicate as it is powerful, like two exquisitely beautiful flowers that don't feed off each other, but are firmly planted in the same soil. Their roots intertwine, they grow together, and they bloom where they're planted! This is no small thing we are talking about, not abstract philosophy—it works! Marriage in its finest sense is fantastic—beyond our noblest descriptions!

Are we overstating it? Absolutely not. Would God have a shabby attitude toward marriage and the human beings *through* whom miraculously and *to* whom trustingly He brings His children into the world? Of course not. He has a warm, balanced formula for its health, and marriages and human beings thrive upon it—and really fantastic things happen:

> I love you not only for what you are,
> but for what I am when I am with you.
> I love you not only for what you have
> made of yourself, but for what you are
> making of me. I love you for the part
> of me that you bring out.
>
> I love you for putting your hand into
> my heaped-up heart, and passing over
> all the foolish and frivolous and weak
> things which you cannot help dimly
> seeing there, and for drawing out

into the light all the beautiful,
radiant belongings that no one else
had looked quite far enough to find.

I love you for ignoring the possibilities of the fool and weakling in
me, and for laying firm hold on the
possibilities of good in me.

I love you for closing your eyes
to the discords in me, and for adding
to the music in me by worshipful
listening.

I love you because you are helping
me to make of the lumber of my life
not a tavern but a Temple, and of
the words of my every day not a
reproach but a song.

I love you because you have done
more than any creed could have done to
make me good, and more than any fate
could have done to make me happy.
You have done it just by being yourself.
Perhaps that is what being a friend
means after all.

It's surely what being happily married means!
Oh, you say, you two are idealists, you're
speaking of something dated and going out of style.
No, no, we don't think so. It better not be. It's real, it's
an essential part of God's plan for the stability of this
world, and we'd better not play games with it. We'd
better not! Don't lose heart, don't forget those silent,
strong multitudes of women who wholeheartedly believe in marriage in its fullest and who have given
their life happily to it only to find themselves whole
and complete and rather holding up a tottering world.

Quite a partnership! Quite a challenge! Quite amazing!

Say that again? Let's join together and say that again and again

. . . and again

. . . and again

. . . and again!

# Six

# Things That Go Bump in the Night

From ghoulies and ghosties
   and long-leggity beasties
And things that go bump
   in the night—Good Lord
   deliver us!
            —*Cornish Prayer*

If you've got a happy marriage going for you, you're not going to spend a lot of time figuring out how it works. We don't think about how our car engine works as long as it does. It's only when we hear some knocks and pings that we think about what's going on under the hood. Even the happiest marriage has its highs and lows—that's life, isn't it? If it's a strong partnership, things usually work out. Sometimes we might not be in tune with our spouse, he's

77

having business problems, or the children or friends or our work is giving us trouble, or someone falls ill, someone close dies, or we're upset by moving or money problems. These are the inevitable crises that all human beings face from time to time. How we deal with them depends on our inner strength and common sense and often our *own* decision as to our attitude toward these things. You know this is everyone's—women's and men's—total last freedom, the freedom to decide their attitude toward *any* circumstance. We can't back out—and, oh, how we all try to. "She made me feel this way," "He made me have a bad attitude," "Those circumstances caused me to be ugly"—no! no! no! She didn't, he didn't, they didn't—*you* did. You *let* them. You turned loose your last freedom, you let go, you swayed with the wind, you *let* your attitude be "had"; when it's *your* possession and *your* responsibility. We must *never* forget that. Often, it seems to us, we get so involved with the everyday human experiences that we forget the real pitfalls of marriage, the ones that are with us all the time, the way the air we breathe is with us. Things we can't see—the things that go "bump" in the night!

We sometimes sense something might be going on, but we don't pay too much attention, and like the air, we don't notice these things too much. But if our lives become too strongly influenced by them, we're brought up short one day by the damage that has been done, slowly but surely, to our marriages and our lives.

We're talking really now about qualities in our twentieth-century lives, about the way our society is organized, what is made to seem important, about the way we react to what's happening, and about assumptions we make. How important it is for us to understand how we think and act, for it's all very well to say we've found a center for our lives in our husbands and families and in the Lord, that we have a framework, but we don't live in a vacuum. The framework is overlaid with the people and events of the world we live in; the wheel—our world—doesn't stand still, but makes its way through both peaceful valleys and rough deserts. And everything has an effect on our marriages and lives. Because it's our world primarily that is undergoing almost unbelievable changes we women need to pay attention to the pitfalls—we have a lot at stake. More is being asked of us, and we are asking for more, while at the same time we want to hold onto the meaningful and wonderful values of marriage and life that every women knows will never change. Women are trying to learn how to balance their desire for personal fulfillment with their natural deep commitment to the many people they love in their lives.

Within a marriage one of the truly glorious aspects is the oneness that grows between a couple. We start out getting married with the idea that it's a perfect relationship that's going to last forever. All too soon, we discover that this thing isn't set on "automatic"—we can set all our electrical appliances on this gauge, but not our marriage. We discover also that there are a hundred rough edges to be smoothed, and that it is really a long walk . . . a grand adventure! No rapid transit system is going to carry you to lasting, unchanging bliss. Unavoidably, our present way of life gives us the false expectations that everything comes to us instantly. When it's a question of switching from quick grits (five minutes in the making) to instant grits (only two minutes!) we go for it—maybe we can use those extra three minutes for something else. Then finally we laugh at ourselves! When we have many demands on our time, instant helps have real value. Instant communication to all parts of the globe, by telephone and by satellite television, opens up new worlds. Computers give us instant answers, making possible feats of achievement no one dreamed of only a couple of decades ago. There is a plane that can take us from New York to Paris in only three and a half hours, there are products on the supermarket shelves that can give us a dinner in fifteen minutes that once might have taken us three hours to prepare. We've got instant celebrities from just one magazine article and instant replays to give us new insights into sports. Our technology is wonderful, truly awe-inspiring, and although perplexing, genuinely beneficial to our everyday lives and to the quality of life.

But it's a pitfall sure enough if we think *instant* always means better. Or that the time we've saved is *always* used to our best advantage. Instant doesn't guarantee anything but quick. Yet we are so accustomed by society to expecting instant fulfillment of all our desires and needs that when we have a problem to solve that takes a careful, tedious, plowing through that no technology can speed up, we are lost, we face a kind of despair and emptiness that nothing can alleviate instantly. We make tragic errors in our endeavors to reach quick solutions, and our marriages and our lives suffer.

We are increasingly aware, nowadays, of the instant Christian, and what is happening here is a model for everything we are saying. Conversion *is* an experience like no other, and it *does* come about in an instant—a decision to change direction, to accept Christ. It is a sudden experience that surely changes a life forever. To be born again can happen in the twinkling of an eye—with an "I will." We make our personal commitment to the Lord, and *then* we begin our new life, our new spiritual pilgrimage. Begin, mind you.

What does not happen is that we become instant authorities. Maybe after years of living as born again Christians (and there is no other kind of Christian may we say here, for there is no other way to become a Christian except to be "born again"—that's what it's about), we will be granted some wisdom, maybe after we have set one foot on the path, and another and another, we will be able to share our knowledge and expound questions of faith. Conversion doesn't give us anything instant except our total confidence in and acceptance of the Lord as our personal Savior and the beginning of our walk in eternal life. The disciples asked Jesus for more, more faith, more revelations, more miracles. "You are still only spiritual babes. You are able to digest the milk and the bread, but you aren't ready for the meat. That takes time."

The person who jumps from a burning building into a net ten stories below is saved, but so is the child who walks out of the same burning building from the ground floor. Both of them have to walk away and keep walking, but in our eagerness for the spectacular and the exciting, we grant the one who jumps some special gift, some special wisdom; we seem to think he's more authentically saved than the child. And we listen, but he can tell us no more, really, than the child. We see a woman espousing radical concepts of womanhood. She is forceful, spectacular, and offers extremist solutions to all the problems of women today. She claims erroneously to be speaking for all women when she has just "jumped" into the spotlight. Some women set her up as a heroine and listen to her pronouncements on all sorts of subjects, while she claims instant answers. Sometimes it takes awhile before the world sees another kind of woman— the woman who walks quietly year after year on her way, arm in arm, with her husband. She can't know anything, the world thinks. Isn't it all too slow to be meaningful? Well, it's slow and meaningful enough to make her some sort of genuine authority sure enough, don't you agree? Her credentials are pretty impressive. The world gets mixed up today on who the authorities really are, and is too quick to overlook that woman who has paid her dues. The genuine article, born out of time, slow and meaningful—like a diamond or a pearl. There is nothing quick about quality. Rembrandt didn't paint by numbers, you know. Nevertheless, that quick solution catches our eye, intrigues us, promises so much, and before we have a chance to see what its consequences are, a new celebrity with a quicker solution has come to replace the first. Is it any wonder that we too often forget about the meat, and gorge ourselves on milk and bread . . . thinking because we are fat we are well fed? One takes a long time in the preparation, the other is ready at hand.

Marriage itself is a commitment, not a contract instantly fulfilled. A contract is instantly completed, signed, sealed, and delivered; a commitment is a lifetime adventure. You may be married in an instant, but then you are only at the beginning of the long walk. The two of you don't become one with the preacher's blessing. The marriage vows don't deal in answers, only the framework, the promises that you are going to spend your life fulfilling.

The fulfillment doesn't come instantly, the real oneness of marriage comes so slowly and quietly, we scarcely know it's happening, and because it's not obvious, some are tempted to be impatient; they're not used to waiting.

"You don't know, at first, how patient you do have to be for oh, so long, until everything falls into place. The fact that we were so much in love carried us through the first years, it seemed to be enough to last forever."

Nancy's ordinary life is the life of many women. She has her husband, her children, her home. And she has the oneness and closeness they worked together to bring about.

"You do become more and more enmeshed in the other person's life, and it seems to me that that's the special talent of a woman. My husband has to travel a lot, and he's out there competing for success, earning a living, dealing with people head to head. He doesn't have the time or energy for the minute and subtle things that women have the time to know.

"When my husband is away, he always calls around six at night. It's kind of a ritual. I remember when I used to be all geared up for that call, because I'd had a terrible day, the kids had been under foot or the washing machine broke down, and I wanted to tell him what a horrible day I'd had and how miserable I felt. That's what a husband was for, to make everything all right, right away.

"Then, once, he stopped me in the middle of pouring out what had happened: 'You know, honey, when I'm away like this, my whole day is geared to evening when I call you, I'm thinking about what I'm going to say to you while I'm shaving or at meetings or seeing customers. And I just want to talk to you so much because I need lifting up while I'm stuck here alone in this hotel room. Let's don't lay the heavy stuff on now. My day hasn't been a lark either.' And it flooded in on me when I stopped to think . . . I've got the familiarity of all the things I love around me, the children, the house, everything, and he has none of that. Instead of supporting him and being sensitive about his needs, I've been putting a lot of unimportant complaining on him, about things I could deal with. But I was looking for sympathy and instant solutions to my problems.

"It occurred to me that sometimes we're more inclined to giving our ear to our children than we are to our husbands. We're too impatient to be heard ourselves, and you can't build closeness if you aren't listening to the other person. I think one of the really important contributions a woman can make to her marriage is to have that ear available to her husband, that kind of sensitive listening he can't get from anyone else. Now, I have time to do that, but even if I had some kind of job with all sorts of problems, I could still be that ear. No one else, not a friend or a brother or a parent shares that oneness or has the same kind of stake in building it up. It's a joint nerve you share, this 'what's affecting you is affecting me.' But what you have to understand, and what I've learned, is that it takes time and effort to get there. It doesn't happen overnight. It's got more depth than the 'quickie' approach could produce."

But overnight, in an instant, we can be shown what it is that we've spent years working at. Martha looks back to a day of crisis, that moment that reveals what it is that we have. Buckner was involved in a serious automobile accident and, critically injured, he spent some twenty-one days in intensive care. Of course everyone rallied around—his family and Martha's and their wonderful church family and people all over the city and even from over the country—and there were many prayers being said. But the worst and most unnerving part was that he wasn't there so that she could talk to him about this terrible thing that had happened, just as they had always shared everything in their life.

*It was really very peculiar. When I was waiting and praying so desperately and earnestly outside the emergency room while they worked to save his life, I felt so deeply the need to tell Buckner what was happening—when he was what was happening! Certainly this was not logical, and I was aware of that, but it was enormously instinctive. Over and over I had this kind of feeling. It was strange and a little tricky, but not unusual according to other women who have shared similar feelings in similar circumstances. Buckner and I had and have always shared immense deep feelings, and this one was so enormous and shocking—that to share this overwhelming feeling with him was so very natural—I missed him terribly!*

We have to give ourselves time, though, to grow up and in to sensitivity. It's all too easy not to make the effort. Like exercise, learning sensitivity can be boring and frustrating; it takes time. That is its price tag. Time. "Instant" has no meaning here. Every human being has some quality or characteristic that another sees as a flaw, and they want to use some sort of instant "correction fluid" to "re-type" somebody. "He could change if he wanted to," a wife will say. "I don't like this or that about him, it's something that affects *my* happiness." Perhaps he simply doesn't squeeze the toothpaste tube right and having your own separate one could solve the whole mammoth problem. Nearly every marriage is worth eighty-nine cents, right?

However, most solutions are not so quick and simple, and they're not possible to solve at all if you're not perceptive enough to see what can be changed and what adjustments must be made. You do have a choice most of the time, you often can work things out . . . you really can.

"When we got married, I just loved to dance, it was one of the things I did well." Carol looked back on eighteen years of marriage and talked about how it had developed into something so wonderful she couldn't have imagined it when she was young. "It seems silly now to think that something like dancing could have been a source of real resentment. My husband was simply reared in a different atmosphere and he never really was around it or liked it. He preferred sports and other activities. That was all there was to it, so he just never learned. I understood that to some extent, but I had no patience, I quietly tormented him because he didn't know how to dance and wouldn't learn. All I could think of was that he was squelching one of my talents by not being out on the dance floor with me. It was doubly hard, because at the time, we were in the military, and one of the most common social activities was a get-together where there was dancing. Well, I would dance with whoever asked me and never stopped to think that my husband wasn't happy to see me off dancing instead of being with him.

"It sounds like a small thing, that little bit of resentment about my husband. But think of how much damage it could have done. The first little nagging thing can turn into a bigger and bigger problem. It's the little 'flaw' that you pick away at while there are more serious problems that you are really talking about.

"All this time, I was growing closer to my husband—I don't for a moment believe that you are as much in love when you marry as you are later—and I was growing up. I began to notice that while he didn't object to my dancing, he wasn't really happy. Not because it was wrong in his eyes, but it divided us. Yet he loved me so much that he wanted me to do what made me happy. Then I thought, 'Do I love him that much?' I knew I did, and as soon as I realized it, I really didn't want to do anything to divide us. I didn't have to dance, it had become first with me. Even if he had encouraged me with his words, I could still sense this thing was a division. Women, you know, are good at sensing things, right?

"You could say I gave up something. No, I wanted to. Well, that was my choice. My marriage was more important to me. Maybe women do have to give up things more often or readily than men. We really don't know that though—that's purely an assumption. If it's something that means a lot, or gives us some kind of distinction, it's not easy to do, and maybe not necessary to relinquish. But that was simply the decision I made. It might seem foolish to some, but each woman decides her priorities, doesn't she? And you have to make some hard choices in life, and you have to understand that nothing happens quickly."

We do believe that nothing in the world worth doing is done instantly, and we women are the ones who have to keep a firm grasp on that knowledge and pass it on to our children. Millie's son, Tyler, saw a toy, a big cuddly bear, that he wanted more than anything. At six, there is nothing like that yearning, and it would have been so easy for Millie to have bought the toy, but instead, she explained to Tyler that he would have to save up his money for the bear—the huge sum of fifteen dollars—by putting dimes and nickles and pennies in his bank until he reached his goal. It was harder on Millie than it was on Tyler, because she had to watch him agonizing as the dollars mounted up. But it was worth it to see the joy in his face the day he arrived at his goal. That bear is a symbol, now. Working to achieve a goal is something that he had to learn at home, because the world in its rush to get things done instantly isn't going to teach him. No sir. Time was when the slow achievement of a goal was a value of society. No longer, yet it's something that individual members of society still see as a great moral value and strength . . . and must keep visible to those coming along behind them. That is a kind of heritage—favor. Martha remembers when she and Buckner first married:

*I always knew somehow that when we married I'd be marrying his books too. He had hundreds of volumes and after these many years of marriage—thousands. And I dearly love books also, but that many, many in a tiny apartment. . . . Oh, you know. Well, he had just ordered a classic set on Abraham Lincoln, which he was paying for monthly, when we married. The statements were being mailed to his parents' address and they would forward them to our new address every month. They were only $6.45 a month, but they were for-e-v-e-r. Just that sum quoted to me now conjures up recollections of for-e-v-e-r. Charlie, Buckner's dad, said, after we'd been married about twenty years, how tempted he was in those early months of our marriage to pay off that small amount. But he felt it was really a good way of finding out early what installment payments are really like. Did it cure us? I'd like to answer that, but I'm laughing too hard. Let me say this—it made us think.*

Children aren't disciplined instantly, and it isn't any fun to do the disciplining. Because mothers spend more time with the children as a rule, it often falls to them to say no, to stop them when they start to get too far out of line. It takes time and effort to remind them what the limits are—there's no such thing as instant character. A young mother we know was in tears because she had to spank her little girl because the child invariably threw a small tantrum each day before going to school.

"She's been spoiled by the family," she said, "and I know she doesn't like sitting still in school, so I finally had to spank her. But I made a mistake. It didn't do any good. She cried the next day just the same. I hate to have to spank her every day . . ."

A spanking every day may not be the solution, but neither is *one* attempt at discipline going to cure a six-year-old and teach her not to throw tantrums. Disciplining is another one of those things that no one has ever found a shortcut for and never will. But all kinds of really tragic mistakes can be made if we rush into making quick decisions about our children because it's the easiest way for us; it halts something we find uncomfortable or embarrassing or painful to us.

Jimmy was a tall and slim, wonderful, loving ten-year-old boy with a super personality, well-adjusted, and a terrific baseball player. "I'm the athlete in the family," he boasted. It was not an empty boast; he was very good at baseball. This pleased his folks a lot because he looked so great in the baseball games. He honored their pride.

Four or five years ago, Jimmy started playing basketball in an athletic program where every child has to be allowed to play, no matter how good or bad he is. Jimmy, his parents quickly learned, was not good. In fact, he was so uncoordinated in that sport, the first thought was that he should stop playing basketball altogether and right away. His performance embarrassed his folks who were very conscious of their own image.

It was his parents' self-centeredness that pushed them toward a quick solution: take him out of athletics and never mind what it might mean to him.

How easy that would have been, until they saw that it was for their sake, not their son's that they were concerned. And that was even more difficult to face. It took them time to see and admit this, but happily they did.

When it became clear that the solution was really long hours of work, helping Jimmy, who so wanted to play, learn how to shoot baskets and showing him the game, it was a revelation for his parents. Patience is hard to come by in teaching if you are accustomed to learning things fast, but the time spent in the backyard with this boy was well worth it. It was a way for him to earn his parents' respect and support his own self-esteem. It taught him staying power, endurance, how to face up to difficulties and the things that don't come easily to him and overcome them. Jimmy can now shoot baskets from anywhere on the court and continues to star in baseball too. He has a good self-image, and he might not have had any of those things if the instant, easy solution had been chosen by the grown-ups responsible for him, because they were worried about their own self-image.

We can all so easily fall into the pitfall of the quick solution, because it's a pervasive quality of the times in which we live. Yet if we turn to the Bible we see that Jesus was never in a hurry, and He accomplished so much in a few short years. One of our favorite and sincerest prayers is that we might have Jesus' *pace* along with His *peace*. Could it not be that they go hand in hand? The pace of our lives is so rapid, too rapid perhaps, that we've lost sight of the sense of accomplishment that a long and time-consuming task can provide. Now, we're all in favor of labor-saving devices, and we don't know that scrubbing the laundry by hand or doing any of the tiresome chores that used to be the lot of women are especially uplifting. But we hate to see accomplishments demeaned by society because they "take time." "What a waste of time," we are too quick to say about an intricate and difficult task of handcraft or domestic work, or things beautifully done by real artisans.

Somehow, if too much is taken away, too much time saved, too many instant solutions take the place of human hands and ingenuity, something of life's meaning is taken away. The long walk does not then have its deserved excitement, it's just plain boring, and meaningless lives are frustrated lives. Frustrated lives seek to spread the tedium and discontent they feel, starting in the marriage and family, and spreading out in circles to friends and acquaintances. Bored lives attract each other like magnets so they can discuss (let's face it—so they can *gossip* about) those whose lives count. It's almost a syndrome. You find it in every facet of society.

The time we are given by labor-saving devices and shortcuts too often becomes empty time, without meaning or sense of accomplishment. We're trapped in a desert of empty time, and we become involved in a desperate search for something to fill it up. Courses in gourmet cooking, flower arranging, tennis lessons, bridge parties, even a job we don't want—doing something we aren't interested in doing—fill up our time because we have to be doing something.

Linda has everything any woman could ask for: a beautiful home, household help, well-behaved children, money to spend, a hard-working husband who is an executive with a large corporation. She wants for nothing, yet she's discontented. She plays tennis regularly, but she doesn't really enjoy it. She belongs to clubs that work for charity, but it's not satisfying. She doesn't have to get up until noon if she doesn't want to, so she doesn't. Her children are al-

ways signed up for activities after school and during
the summer.

Linda's husband would like to move to another
city so that he could rise in management—he's gone as
far as he can where he is—yet Linda refuses. She
wants to stay where she is, doing the same old things,
without comprehending that the person who makes it
all possible deserves the opportunity to find the most
congenial work and conditions, and strangely enough,
she can't seem to comprehend either how empty her
life is, just why she's so discontented. She's bored and
apathetic; and he's being driven away from her because they've lost the feeling of "what's affecting you
is affecting me." It is here, we believe, that having a
strong spiritual framework such as we discussed earlier is so important. Granted, our society gives us free
time; but time with meaning, with the purpose and
concern that the framework gives you, is never wasted
in apathy and boredom. If you are supported within
by a strong spiritual purpose then all of life takes on
an amazing meaningfulness. Even when you're involved in purely social activities that on the surface
are scarcely world-changing you still know that none
of the time is wasted. Perhaps you will have an opportunity to share with others something that has helped
you, or in some other way you might make that day
meaningful. Maybe you can be a willing listener in
that special atmosphere of fun as well as a conscien-
tious friend who cares, and those qualities always
liven up any activity even if it appears to be shallow
on the surface. Simply, you have a more dynamic purpose in "all things." Even fun is more fun! And having
real fun is a good and necessary relief from the pressures of this world. The Lord tells us in His Word that
"a merry heart doeth good like a medicine." We don't
mean that you go out and get on a soapbox and try to

turn their lives around in an instant to be like yours. Of course not. But you are fulfilling a greater purpose—an eternal one. You may perhaps open a door. If you really understand that the Lord can and does work through you to touch many lives, the life you live is never empty. Now this idea is too presumptuous for human beings to have thought up, yet it's a fact of the Scriptures that this is God's way of doing things. He reaches human beings through human beings. We both have been touched by the Lord through hundreds of people. It just happens, many times unconsciously; yet knowing this is an amazing assurance. From then on, nothing is empty time, ". . . for it is God who works in you, inspiring both the will and the deed, for His own chosen purpose."

To us, there is no better answer to the maladies of our times than a spiritual one. Without it, it is like trying to quench a thirst without water. It can't be done. You can try all sorts of thirst quenchers—apple juice, grapefruit juice, orange juice—but you can't spend your whole life with them. You need clean, fresh water. You can fill up your life with tennis and clubs and courses and crafts and cooking, and they may stop your thirst for a while, but they are not a deep-flowing well that never runs dry.

"I will give you living water," Jesus said, "and anyone who drinks this water will never thirst again." Oddly enough, Jesus spoke those words to a woman, a woman of Samaria whom He met at Jacob's Well, whose water was hallowed by tradition and an ancient faith. But Jesus shows her that the water she draws from the well has been replaced by the new water of the Spirit that He is offering. That's the kind of sustaining water that we need today, that gives us meaning, joy, and patience, and if we drink of it, we will never thirst again. Martha's Lisa was very taken with this Scripture when they were in Israel on their way to Jacob's Well. They had read the Scripture aloud before going . . .

*The trip from Jerusalem was rather long and eight-year-old Lisa was wanting to stop all the time for a Coke. Finally we were all very weary with this and Buckner said, "Lisa, you're always thirsty—you've got to work on that, really!" Kids love to stop, you know, everywhere along the way. She then decided that the solution for her was to drink lots and lots of Jacob's Well water, and upon her saying this Buckner and I and her brothers all chimed in to tell her that only a sip might be best because of the change in water. She was adamant and replied, "No, Dad, you ought to be glad. This will solve my problem—totally, for Jesus said that if I drink of this water, I will never thirst again!" She certainly remembered every line of that to get her point across (children always do!)—and now several years later she's been better able to understand what Jesus meant and to translate that Scripture to her own heart very personally.*

One thing we can be sure of, though, is that the water, or satisfaction, or meaning can't be bought, and here's another pitfall of our lives today. Once when Buckner was speaking to the pastor of a small, very poor church in Eastern Europe, he said, "When we return to our church, we'll get some money together to help you. Many of our people will be so concerned, they will want to have a part in your ministry, and you can be certain that we will all pray for you in your need."

The pastor looked at him for a moment and answered, "I've been to America and I've seen the affluence. Our poverty is a tremendous problem, but I believe America's affluence gets in the way of spiritual values perhaps even more. Please pray for us in our poverty and we shall pray for you in your affluence." Buckner and Martha have continued to be touched by this man's statement. He's right, you know, we have to learn how to behave spiritually in both situations—in affluence and in poverty. Or, as the Apostle Paul said, he had learned "to abound and to be abased." That is some great thing to learn!

The affluence of America is a fact of our lives. There are those many who have it, those who are seeking it desperately, those who don't have it and may never, yet see it all around them and crave it. We take our affluence as a nation as our right, and as that pastor well knew, we need prayer to save us from it.

We women are often the keepers of the purse, and we can so easily fall into the trap of using money to fill up the emptiness that can enter a life. Yet we fail to respect what money represents. A young Sunday School teacher, trying to be up-to-date with her class of five-year-olds, told the story of the widow who gave her last two mites to the Lord to show how much she loved Him. Now since a "mite" was the smallest currency in value for that day, the teacher, trying to make the lesson meaningful and applicable, tried to update it. To the children, the teacher said, "She gave her last two pennies." A little boy in the back of the room leaned back in his chair, folded his hands behind his head like a totally confident bank executive, and blurted out, "What's He going to do with a lousy two cents?" It was one of those moments of hilarity, but it reveals a syndrome of our kids today. They have trouble seeing beyond the currency to the meaning. They are little materialists at five-years-old—victims already.

We seem to have lost the sense of the proper

place of money, even our children have lost it. It's the amount of money given and not the gift of love that they see given far too often today. How you view money says a lot about the kind of person you are: For some, money is to be hoarded, for some it is to be used, and sometimes it uses people, and they are hardly ever aware of how. All materialists are not rich—although many are—yet people without money sometimes think that all rich people are materialists. No, you don't have to have money to love it dearly. Materialists come all ways—the rich who worship money and people so greedy for wealth they don't have that they are dying for it. They're just as miserable as those who have it, hoard it, and have no joy of it.

"I think I learned what 'filthy rich' meant when I was still in grade school," remarked one of our friends, who looks back to a poor childhood, but is now well-off as the wife of a prominent lawyer. "There was a girl in my class with really unkind eyes—I'll never forget how cold they were—who was rich, compared to us, and miserable. I don't know that she was miserable because she was rich, but being rich certainly brought out the worst. She used to buy big bags of penny bubble gum, and none of the rest of us could afford even that. And you know, she never shared a single piece with us. Never. I guess she wasn't a likable person to begin with, and this bubble gum thing was just another way of showing the poverty of her spirit; but I decided then and there that if I were ever rich, I was going to buy a ton of bubble gum and throw it around in the street for everybody. I wasn't going to be stingy with anything I had. I know she grew up to be miserable too. Her marriage didn't last, and she's still rich and pitiable. And alone . . . and still has that selfish attitude, I'm sure."

One of the wealthiest men in the history of our country, who made more money than any one human being could ever spend, never used his wealth to benefit the less fortunate, although he once consented to make a donation to charity in another's name. He wrote a check for six dollars. We cannot help but wonder at the spiritual poverty that was shored up by millions of dollars.

There is a story about a woman who was given a check for a large sum, and when she took it to the bank to cash it, the teller said, "You've forgotten to endorse this."

So the woman wrote on the back of the check, "I wholeheartedly endorse this check." Astonished, he said, "I know you're all for it, lady, but you have to sign your name!"

It's so easy to endorse what we believe to be the good things in life, but a lot of people won't sign their name to it and commit themselves. We sign the checks and take the cash, but we spend it unwisely. Money has become a symbol of so many things to us, a testing ground between men and women, of "my" money and "your" money, and a reflection of our character and our ideas about money as we grew up. Ken and Millie sit down together every month and pay the bills. He writes the checks, she does the envelopes and files them. Although Millie could have her own account, she prefers to write checks from their joint account.

*Ken and I have had many "discussions" about how money was to be used in our marriage. I felt it was to be used freely as long as it lasted without a great deal of thought as to what was essential and what was not. I did not have an abundance of money as I grew up, but still my attitude was such that you spent what you*

*had and then did the best you could until you got
some more! Fortunately for us, this was not Ken's philosophy regarding money. He felt you should plan
carefully all your expected expenditures and be very
practical. So every month when we sat down to write
out our monthly bills, it was always a lively occasion.
I remember one night in particular when we started
our "bill-paying" session. Ken took out a little cartoon
he had found in some magazine and presented it to
me. It pictured this haggard-looking man sitting at his
desk, piled with bills, and a rather stern-looking
woman standing by the desk looking down at him.
The man is saying, "No, Millie [Ken had changed the
name], I don't want to take it with me—I just want it
to last till I go." We realized that we had different
feelings concerning money and we could see the humor even in our differences and we tried not to let
these differences divide us.*

In regard to feelings about money, sometimes
women have been made to feel of late, that if you
don't provide a product, if you don't get paid a salary
by an employer, that the money earned by the breadwinner is a gift, unearned, not hers by right for pro-
viding the valuable, essential service of household man-
ager. Too many women who have devoted hours and
lives to creating a home and comfort and raising children have been swayed by a wind blowing through
society that says paid services are the only jobs with
status. Yet we know that's not true. The total picture
has been confused by the issue of equal pay and the
right of women to work if they choose. The intangible
services of running a home—not just the specific tasks
of cleaning and cooking and clothing a family, but the
priceless gifts of love and understanding, of the ear
that listens to an infant's cry, a teen-ager's youthful

agonies, a husband's triumphs or defeats—can't have a price tag, no matter how loudly the voices in the marketplace sound. Money is power, we agree, but it is the power of the world beyond the home. Within the home, there is greater power, greater strength, in a wife's love, in a mother's touch. We need not so much to be raised up out of the so-called drudgery of being a homemaker as to raise ourselves up and reveal the wealth that our contentment gives us.

A woman was being chided for
feeling her particular gift was
homemaking
"I wouldn't do that for all the money
in the world," said the cynic
"Neither would I," she replied, with
a smile and
a knowing look.

# Seven

# But I _Thought_ You Meant...

"I thought you meant . . ." "I just assumed . . ."

Have you ever said that? Of course you have, we all have. It's a very human failing, making assumptions. We all tend to assume things about one another by not really communicating our honest feelings. We are particularly vulnerable to doing this in marriage, and if we're not careful, our assumptions take over rather than the _real_ feelings involved. So many times we don't ask the direct question, or we remain silent, "assuming" the other person, the one we think we know so well, will understand what we really mean. We're feeling things, maybe, that we never bother to mention, or perhaps we are hesitant to. We women especially tend to lean on our intuition, a good and valuable quality surely, but intuition is only a guide. It can't give us all the answers. We can use our intuition to help us ask the right questions, to help us uncover hidden meanings, but we should never make the mistake of depending on it alone, letting it put words or thoughts into the mouth and mind of another.

We can't think of anything that's more important in a marriage than communication. In fact, most marriage counselors agree that when this indispensable quality goes out of a marriage, hope for reconciliation is very slim. Communicating allows us to avoid making assumptions that can lead to great unhappiness and sometimes complete misunderstanding. It can resolve resentments that might have grown and grown in silence until the relationship was irreparably damaged. Really communicating allows us honestly to know and understand each other, and this is vital in marriage: If we are one, as the Lord said, then for one half of us to be out of touch with the other half really divides us *inside*, too.

We grow up making assumptions. We begin very early in life, as children. We thought a few more inches in height would make us all grown-up in every sense. Aunt Suzy with the biggest house and most expensive possessions was bound to be the happiest relative (she wasn't!). Or Uncle Jeb who was always sick-looking was the most spiritual (he wasn't, either). Or that money could solve everything, or that becoming an adult would be a lark—all sorts of things! But time and maturity and experience began to teach us so much. We found out they were not static; neither are we—we're still learning, we haven't stopped "assuming." It's only when we've lived a good many years that we even begin to put away our childish assumptions and begin to understand what really makes us grown-up: the strong internal props, the values that we trust and know as right.

The old assumptions of childhood, though, are

so often replaced by new ones. We have a husband whom we love. We believe we're perceptive about his thoughts and needs, we assume we know what he likes, what he wants from us. After all we know him pretty well. Yet we both have heard women say, "My husband wouldn't want me to do that," or "He'd never let me wear a dress like that." Ah, has he told you so? we ask. "No," they answer, "but I know he wouldn't like it." These women so clearly want to, very much, but their assumptions hold them back. They hold them back from even expressing their desires, their real feelings, to the man who is their partner in life! And some of them, never having worn the dress of their dreams, hide a little seed of resentment, one that can easily grow into something truly damaging.

What every woman must understand too is whether her assumption is valid or whether she's using it as an escape for herself.

Claire had dropped out of nursing school to marry, and nearly twenty years later her children were grown and independent. It was her heart's desire to return to nursing school and finish what she had begun as well as giving her in her later years a valuable occupation for which she had a talent.

"I'd go," she said, "but Ed wouldn't like it."

"Now, how do you know that? Have you talked about it?"

"No, we haven't discussed it, but I know Ed. He'd hate the idea."

Claire built up a big case against Ed in her mind. He was almost the enemy, because she assumed that he wouldn't like the idea of her returning to school. The idea meant so much to her but she just couldn't bring herself to tell him, not for a long time. And the day she got the courage and said, "I know you won't want me to do this, but . . ." was the day the foolishness of making assumptions came home to her.

"I'd be so proud of you if you'd do that," he said.

"I wasted years," she said later, "because I just assumed that he'd be against it. And I think I made the assumption partly because of myself. I was a little afraid to commit myself at my age to going back to school. I used Ed as an excuse and as a 'cop-out,' kinda. But I also really thought he'd have a negative reaction. It horrifies me to think what a trick I played on us all. To think that after all the years we've been married I could have missed the very quality in him that would think it was a wonderful idea."

We know that we make a lot of assumptions about strangers, but we often forget that it happens right under our nose. No matter how much we seem to talk, assumptions come about when there's no communication in those words . . . or when what we say is not what we mean.

A good example is Sally, a young woman in her late twenties, who was quite heavy and dressed like a woman three times her age. "I'd love to slim down and wear a really slinky dress," she said, "but my husband wouldn't stand for me to do that. He likes me the way I am." But she didn't like the way she was, and her assumption that he liked her that way was not true of how he really felt. Her longing to change finally led her to confront him with that assumption, and when the lines of communication opened up, she found that he did not "like" her overweight and dowdy, but he had had difficulty too expressing such a feeling—and when they began communicating, he admitted something else too: He had a deep insecurity about himself and really feared that if she made herself attractive, he would lose her to another man.

"That was ridiculous," she said. "But if I'd allowed us to go on too much longer with all our assumptions, I think he might have lost me sure enough, maybe not to another man, but to my own feelings of frustration, for we were in different worlds."

Now Judy's assumptions were different indeed, but very exhausting! She has only been married a few years now, but she recalls that the first few months of married life were very tiring to her. Both she and her husband worked, but she raced home each night to have a big dinner on the table the minute he walked through the door forty-five minutes after her.

"I just assumed that he thought that was what a wife was supposed to do. I even imagined how angry he'd be if I didn't, and I went even further to set up my argument back to him. I never asked him, I just did it, and if I didn't have the dinner ready on the dot, I felt terribly guilty. It was really silly. Then one day I told him, almost angrily, I just couldn't keep it up day after day. I really built up a case. He laughed, and said he had never expected me to. In fact, he was about to suggest that I take it easy. I was astonished—really, truly shocked! That taught me a lesson; every time I start doing something because I assume it's what he wants, I make sure it really *is* something he wants or expects. This has really made a remarkable difference I can hardly describe!"

A real effort at communicating can solve so many problems in a marriage, large and small. You risk nothing by setting things straight, yet you risk your marriage if you don't. Silence is only golden when it's not also a wall. We all have so many aspects of our personality that we never bring out into the open, but they can be sources of conflict with those who are dearest to us, with those we think we know best. Well, let's get practical about this. How is communication nourished? What are some of its essential needs? Perhaps you feel it's been dulled in your marriage. What to do? Well, the first big hurdle is to stop "assuming" it'll all work out, recognize the need, and get with it in this vital area. How? By sheer planning and making "getting back in touch" your top priority. Nothing is more important—nothing—if your marriage is weak here.

Let's talk about husbands and wives. Do you and your husband still "date"? We mean do you go out to dinner by yourselves and plan a really cozy evening for the two of you, to just talk and gaze into each other's eyes and heart? Do you take the effort and time to communicate? To communicate in an atmosphere where you can? Oh, you say, you're living on "cloud nine"—when you're married, you settle down. To what? A "yawny" dull routine? Oh, we hope not. That's double dreary, not only because it's so boring, but because—and here's the biggie—*you* bring that on yourself. You're the culprit. As Pogo once said in that terrific cartoon: "We have seen the enemy—and it is US!" You don't have to live like that. Not really. Having time alone together as a couple has got to be—in a good marriage. You both need it, and we think that every woman *still* knows this. Perhaps men know it too, we know for sure our husbands do. Anyway, suppose you feel and act on the "premise" that your husband doesn't agree or won't do this, or that your childrens' schedules must come first always? Have you really talked together about it and paid the price in communication? We used the word *premise* because it's an amazing thing the way both men and women presume sometimes what the other thinks. Lots of women take a "doormat" role because they presume that's what their husband wants, when in reality he may have married a very charming, confident woman in the beginning who got lost in the process by her own assumptions. He will always respect you *more* if you're the *you* he once knew, not the "blah" you've let him take the brunt for creating. *You* did that—*you* can change that. Communicate! We once heard of a very rigid man who told his wife every move to make and even every cosmetic not to use, even not to use deodorant. She dutifully followed along, and lost her self-esteem and her husband's—he ran off with another woman! Now who was to blame? *Both.* He had no business overlording it, and she had no business remaining silent. Communication would have taken care of it if real love was there. He might have realized how ridiculous were his requests if she'd been strong enough to balk and talk, and he'd surely have respected her and seen her in a new way. Emerson said in effect that we only get as much respect as we demand, and this woman demanded none. If you like that kind of existence (it's certainly not really living), OK, but the path is strewn with broken ties and broken hearts. So that word that speaks volumes—COMMUNICATION—is a priceless commodity in marriage, and why not, when the origin of its meaning is "common union"—a strong description of what marriage is all about.

But you say what about my children and their needs? Well, what about them? How can you combine those necessary husband-wife rendezvous and your childrens' needs? Have you told your children you both need this time together and helped them to understand, too, so that they'll do the same when they're married? Aren't schedules give and take anyway? Sometimes, many times, we change our plans because of our childrens' schedules, and they must be led to do the same when it is possible. All of life is give and take; sometimes the light is green, sometimes red—you adjust that's all. And you *must* find time for whatever preserves your relationship—*must!* Every woman knows a woman has many relationships; she knows this as a wife, mother, daughter, and sometimes career woman, too. Daily she has confrontations with people on every level in shopping and managing the household. She's equipped to handle all these relationships if she pays the price of time, communication, the figuring of priorities, and lovingly some give and take.

Let's look at some of the other touchy areas when it comes to assumptions. Money, as we mentioned earlier, is one of the tricky items in life. It represents so much more than cash in the bank or to be spent. We assume that the person we married feels the same way about money as we do. What we forget, very often, is that our attitudes toward money were shaped a long time ago with the way our family treated it. Thus, if we come from a family where money was used to buy experiences—trips and adventures, visits to new and interesting places—and we marry a man whose family believes that money should be put away for a rainy day, we may be puzzled or hurt when the two heritages meet head on. Perhaps every extra penny they had was saved up to send a large family through college. He's not necessarily going to express his attitude in words, but she sees only that he's tucking more than enough into the bank and fusses about paying the bills (possibly the way his father did, but she can't always know that). Or maybe he seems to spend far too much and he never seems to worry. But maybe her family paid their bills the day they arrived and she remembers it down deep and nags him nervously. There are a thousand variations and a million little conflicts when it comes to money. How easy it would be to sit down and talk about why each feels as he or she does about money, and to resolve to make adjustments so that each feels comfortable. And how hard it is to analyze our own past and admit that we just might be a little unreasonable. Money is really a sensitive area, and those in the "know" say it represents affection—that's something to think about.

"I finally realized," one of our friends said, "that my husband's bad temper and predictions of poverty at bill-paying time were bred into him by his father, who was an accountant and, besides that, lived through the Depression with almost no money. Of course his attitude was entirely logical, and we talked about it, and how he's making plenty of money now and can afford to take it a little easier about it. He's never going to change completely, but it clears the air. I used to get so angry with him, but now, I think we at least understand what's going on."

We need perceptiveness and sensitivity to talk about many areas like money where we haven't usually made conscious decisions about how we deal with them, but unconscious ones planted deep in us by our backgrounds. Just knowing this fact is certainly a beginning factor in communicating when it comes to money.

Our emotional relationship, and sex in particular, is another area that needs to be kept healthy and happy. How's your sex life? What's it like? How are you communicating in this area? Now, we're not at all interested here in a "sex manual" kind of answer, a description of positions and procedures. These approaches can surely stir up the animal instincts, but that powerful and treasured commodity—LOVE—is lost somewhere in the process. In fact, no one's wanting a verbal answer at all. Whose business is it but yours and your husband's anyway? But you have to know that it *is your business* and it's very important to have a real and honest look at it from within your heart. As someone once perceptively said, "It's not the position but the disposition that makes men and women happy!" We're talking about sex life as blossoming in deep love between you and your husband. There's nothing like that. Oh, you say, you are enthusiastic Christian women—you mean s-e-x means something to you? You'd better believe it, and if you've read the statistics lately, the experts seem to have discovered that by far the most responsive women in this area are deeply religious. Why should people be surprised? Sex without guilt within marriage with the man of your dreams is like it's supposed to be—super, warm, and most creative. *Creative*—that's a good word, isn't it? In God's plan the sexual experience is given the honor of being the vehicle for creation as well as the joy of the created. As the lovely song so aptly says: "God thought of everything." It's a beautiful, dynamic, exciting experience between husband and wife, an exquisite gift from God that should be treated with its deserved delights and delicacies, and should always be given its honored and rightful respect, regardless of the harsh ways the world uses it and buys and sells it in the marketplace. It deserves better and wasn't meant to be treated casually or tawdrily, but majestically, because within its God-planned rightful setting—marriage—God not only backs it, but gives it to us as a superwonderful, invigorating, and enchanting gift!

Even the happiest marriage, though, has moments when silence and assumptions about sex take the place of openness and communication. It does no good for you to say, "We will communicate in this area or that area, but we can't talk about sex, what bothers me, what pleases me, what you think and feel." No two people are ever going to be exactly in tune all the time, no two people have the same feelings. But it's a mistake to assume your spouse understands completely what's in your mind; it's equally a mistake to assume that you know what's in his. We can't afford not to be open, not to learn to respond honestly, not to talk when we might erase misunderstanding, change an attitude, or resolve an uncertainty. Even in this day when sex is spoken of so openly, there remains still lots of silence on the subject in many modern marriages. Many women still feel shy and reluctant to discuss it even with their husband, and instead, they make assumptions that may well be quite incorrect. Strangely enough, some women really equate their shyness with a kind of virtue, and that's not right at all, for God intends that we certainly should be communicative with our husband in this very sensitive area of our deep emotions. We certainly should drop all assumptions here at all costs and work to develop a warm comfortable communication in this area, for God ordained this for our joy and for our good. Why, genuine sexual pleasure is one of the most beautiful forms of communicating in itself. How can one *not* communicate and communicate at the same time? Husbands and wives must relate here. There are hundreds of books that talk about sex nowadays, and we're overwhelmed by sex in so many ways, television, movies, books, magazines. In some ways, this exploitation would make one think that sex is the only and most important part of marriage and life. A sensible person knows that this is not so. But we know, too, that it is vitally important in marriage and is definitely in God's design to make marriage beautiful and delightful. We know that some couples do have serious problems in their marriage that have to do with sex, and they do need help in this very vital area. No question about it. We can't do better than suggest experienced counseling for such couples if communication seems to have broken down completely.

So we wonder how many marriages have failed because of a problem with communication about sex. We wonder how many men have failed to see a response in their wife and have assumed that there is no caring because there's only silence. We wonder, too, how many women have made some pretty big assumptions about what their husband wants and have resorted to playacting and manipulation because they've been ill-advised that it will save their marriage. And how many of them have found themselves no better off . . . and with even less esteem. We wonder.

There are no gimmicks or tricks or shortcuts. There is only sensitivity and communication. And fortunately one of the most powerful gifts women have, if they'll use it, is sensitivity—seeing the need for communication where it's broken down. Your husband may know this too, but please try to really see him, and see that in his pressures, his sometimes insurmountable binds, his incredible responsibilities, he may be so preoccupied and weary with tension that he can hardly think past his immediate demanding deadlines. He'd surely welcome a warm touch of the human spirit from you—*communicate*—that's a lovely gift when delicately shared. A wise woman knows that it is her job to sense a problem; she is a real guardian of the intangibles of a marriage, the emotional climate, the good and bad feelings, the sense of security that binds the two of you close. No manipulation of desire and needs can replace genuine undestanding and real communication. Each of us, men and women, have our distinct and unique roles in this area of communication. Women, take a look at your husband's world. It's strong and productive and masculine, and yours is equally meaningful and feminine. God forbid we lose those distinctions. Life won't back that—and we'll breed in the future, if we breed at all, weaklings in both sexes who don't know who they are! Too much of that is already happening; we must see it for what it is and know that "neuter genders" are not in God's plan. We are distinct and special and individual in our own ways and we each have our innate ways of communicating with each other.

There's still another kind of silence, another kind of lack of communication that's a little harder to describe. It's the lack of communication with ourselves, the kind that comes, many times, from guilt, unresolved guilt. That is the most destructive thing you can carry around with you. In a sense, it is part of the condition of humankind, the consciousness of sin and falling short that all human beings have. You can accept that fact or not—it's still a fact. It's like walking along and falling into a hole. You can deny you're in the hole, you didn't dig the hole, you didn't want to be in the hole, but you still are in the hole and need to get out. Then someone comes along and says, "I will get you out of this hole." Now, you have a choice either to get out of the hole or to stay there, but to get out, you have to take the Hand that's stretched out. All you have to do is admit to yourself and to that One with the outstretched hand that you want to get out.

This disturbance in the conscience that we call guilt is part of the human condition, although not all people will admit it, and many try to drown it out with noise or playacting. The uncomfortableness somewhere in the spirit can be resolved by reaching out to communicate with God; it is His hand that is outstretched to help you from the hole you once denied existed. To be born again means that guilt is removed, you are at home with God. Guilt carried around can make us ill and irascible, can make us critical of others because we see in them flaws that we don't admit in ourselves. When guilt is removed, we aren't forever sinless, we are learners and we make mistakes still, but the line of communication with oneself and with God has been opened.

We human beings carry around many degrees of guilt beyond the sense of spiritual unease that Jesus redeems us from. Events occur and hidden guilts are exposed. How tragic it is when a couple loses a child and instead of turning to each other for support, they turn against each other, sometimes secretly because each feels guilty, each feels, perhaps, that God is punishing her or him for something. God does not take away a child to punish the living. He doesn't send a retarded child to punish you. He doesn't cause bad things to happen just to spank you. But if you feel that way, it's time to look closely at the reason why, before the guilt that gives rise to such feeling tears apart your marriage and really upsets your life. Jesus came to lift us out of that hole, to erase our guilt, and to give us what He so wonderfully described as abundant life! His life-erasing power makes this possible! And it's not exclusive, it's for "whosoever will."

God has given us a solution; it requires that we break the silence within ourselves that keeps us from admitting our sense of guilt . . . by admitting simply our need for forgiveness. Don't feel that you're the only one who needs forgiveness; every living human being does. The vertical relationship with God can be restored; we can put aside our guilt and gain spiritual peace . . . "peace that passeth all understanding." But, you say, I have trouble forgiving myself. Everyone seems to have this trouble and God, as usual, has a word for us here when He tells us, ". . . If your

heart condemns you, God is greater than your heart!"
He can take care of all of our needs. In short, He is
wanting us once again to follow Him. He forgives us—
we must too. There's energy here, because God is in
it!

So in this very sensitive area of communication,
it must sometimes become quite personal for us to be
able to communicate with others. One thing communication does not allow is that one be inert. Passivity
won't get it. You have to be strong and willing and
aggressive—it's that important. You accept forgiveness
just as aggressively as you give it. This victorious en-
ergetic life just doesn't fall in our lap; we must have
"get up and go" and assert ourselves in the name of all
the best things in life. For in every facet of life, the
more energy and effort we exert, the more benefits
follow. As the old saying suggests: "Good fortune,
oddly enough, belongs to the man who works the
hardest." But, you say, "Remember the song 'The Best
Things in Life Are Free'?"—the moon, the stars, the
robin that sings? Absolutely, but do we take the time
to look at them, absorb them, examine them, let them
speak to our souls? They're free, except for the price
of the time we give to really enjoy them; and for some
people, that's a price they are not willing to pay. So,
they miss the moon, the stars, the robins, the dreams.
They seem to want all the best things to assault them
aggressively without any effort on their part, without
any effort at communication—it won't happen. The
Irish say it so cleverly: "A man would have to keep his
mouth open a long, long time before a roast pheasant
would fly into it." We need always to communicate, to
be aware, reaching out, putting forth our best efforts,
paying the price, whatever, for the good life with our
loved ones, the *best* things in life . . . which are
brought about by really expressing our deep feelings,

emotions, and tenderest love. This is an enchanting job, not an automatic thing. Work! Work! Work!

God gives the birds their food, but
He does not throw it into their nests.
—*Greek Proverb*

Somehow, most women *still* know this!

# Eight

# You're Beautiful!

So, we've got the perfect answer to almost every problem—communication, talking it out, saying how and what we feel, honestly. Well, it's almost perfect. Honesty has a couple of hidden perils we sometimes forget. We hear a lot about it these days, but not enough, we think, about its consequences. We women know that a few simple words can have tremendous power—in our marriage, in dealing with our children, in friendships, and really for all kinds of people, known and unknown, to whom we speak all throughout our lives. It's power that can do great good or bring harm; honesty works both ways. It can build someone up or it can tear that person down.

In Berkley's school, there is a motto pinned on the walls of the classrooms: "Is it true? Is it kind? Is it necessary?" How good it would be if the parents of all the fourth- and fifth-graders who see the sign every day always asked *themselves* the same three questions before they opened their mouth to be honest. If the answer to all three is yes, there's one more question: "Will you be responsible to make your statement clear?" You can smother or starve an idea in words, you know? We can overtalk or even undertalk and not be *clear*. The main responsibility we have in using words is to clearly say what we believe must be said, not with insinuations or vague questions left. We must be careful to have our facts straight, use our words with honesty and conviction, and when dealing in problems or personalities, aim for that redemptive quality that words can bring about. So often we talk about very vital things involving a person's entire life and reputation with such incoherency and unknowledgeable ramblings that we "muddy" the waters. We never realize that the part of valor is to be courageous enough to take full responsibility for what we say, and be *really* up front, clear, and redemptive. We're held just as responsible for throwing hurtful words around ignorantly about people as we are for physically stoning them. We women can't escape this responsibility. We deal so much of the time in just the currency of words, that we speculate, we talk a situation over and over, we examine the ins and outs of personalities, problems, and possibilities without a thought to our powerful tools—words. The freedom and opportunities we have to communicate carry with them a real responsibility to use our gift wisely.

*Is it true?* How often we have heard people remark, "Can't we be honest here?" And we instinctively say, "Yes, we're supposed to tell the truth." Honesty is a virtue. Truth is important. Maybe it's true, all right, when you say to a friend, "You have the most obnoxious way of chewing gum." But the truth may ruin your friendship and probably won't cure her of the way she chews gum. It may be true when you tell your child, "You're the worst speller in the whole family," but no sensitive mother would dream of expressing that very harsh truth to an eager ten-year-old. Maybe it's true that your husband is losing his hair or isn't as slim as he once was. Your mother and father are getting old and forgetful, and Dad repeats the same old stories over and over again. You've never liked your best friend's hairstyle, and you really do not care for the colors she's used to decorate the brand-new living room she's so proud of. Maybe all those things are true facts or true expressions of your feelings. Are they things you're going to communicate in the name of honesty and truth? No, of course not. It's almost ridiculous to use such examples. No woman, unless she is setting out to injure another deeply, would come out and say these things. Yet there are many cases where a few words spoken in "honesty" are equally hurtful, but it's not so obvious that they will be.

What we're trying to point out is that everything we say to another ought to be filtered through our sensitivity and tested by our understanding of our own motives for saying it—and by our real *caring* about the situation. Just because something is true, and just because there is a great outcry against hypocrisy and for complete honesty these days, doesn't mean that we put aside all kindness and all restraint. In fact, honesty itself is sometimes used hypocritically, for many people confuse honesty with repentance, and really try to make it a virtue. For example, we've heard people say, "Well, I know I'm catty, but that's just the way I am." And they feel all "clean and pure" after saying that, when they've not changed one thing and they plan to continue their cattiness. Just being honest about ourselves does not do a thing to change us until we also plan to make some changes. Women have always known how much words can do. They can tear down friendships, a marriage, a loving relationship with parents or children. Words have always been one of our weapons of defense or of aggression, where men have had guns and swords, and other kinds of power. But it seems to us that each woman should realize anew this gift and strength, and that used with restraint and sensitivity, she can do great good. If she will take the time to talk things out, details that women are so at home with—that look so wordy to the nontalker—are not all that bad if they correct a misrepresentation or erase a false impression.

*Is it necessary?* Some things have to be said, though. The truth that we know can hurt, sometimes must hurt for good ends. Now, here is where courage enters. It does not take courage to gossip—no way— but it takes great courage to do redemptive talking. For example, to speak when we know that when we open our mouth what we have to say isn't going to make either the listener or speaker happy. But if we profess to hold to certain principles and moral values, or if we feel strongly beneath our anger or annoyance that another person has to hear something necessary, then we have to speak.

Jane had just come home from a meeting of a group of neighborhood women who get together regularly to exercise, plan schedules for car pools, shared baby-sitting, and other activities, and she's depressed.

"I had to give Sandy a piece of my mind this morning, and I feel just terrible. But I had to do it, that group is so important to all of us, and her destructive complaining and wriggling out of responsibilities is ruining everything for the rest of us. Nobody else would say anything, though everyone has been hurt and has been fuming for a long time. There was a lot of talking behind her back, but that didn't do any good at all. It never does. So I finally told her what was being felt. I *did* do the right thing, I know that, but I think I did it in the wrong spirit—that's so important, too.

"The trouble is, it's not because what I said was untrue, or that she shouldn't have been told. What I feel troubled about is that I didn't say it with love. I did it in an angry way and used it to get out a lot of bad feelings I had about her. And that was not right. I could have brought peace out of this situation, but I didn't take time to talk it through. I was hasty.

"I called her later, and said, 'Sandy, I can't say that I'm sorry for what I said, but I do want to apologize for the manner in which I said it. I still feel what I said was exactly right, I stand by that, but I *am* sorry for saying it in that really hostile way. Let's talk some more, our friendship is too important for short-cuts.'

"Telling truths like that are hard to do and are hurtful enough, but kindness can take the edge off. I learned a lot. I learned that both telling her the truth and then having to apologize for my bad attitude took great strength, and for me that was a good lesson on how redemptive words require great courage."

We women are so often the ones who must say necessary but not necessarily pleasant things. And we take the blame for the hurt. Our children wouldn't respect us for long if we failed to speak out and remind them of unpleasant truths. It's no fun to say no, it's no fun to say a lot of things that are just part of a mother's responsibility. Yet it is from their mother who is with them almost constantly from the very beginning of their life that children must begin to learn about what is true and right—those essential moral principles that we want them to hold. Fathers play a vital role of course, and more and more as the babies grow, but somehow "mother" is cast into a heavy role very early, and she had better know from the outset that her children hear her "vibes" *more* than her words. And our teaching is so often in terms of practical applications, restraints, and encouragements we offer our children, which sometimes aren't exactly what they had in mind. We have only our best judgments to follow, but we can make our vision of truth stick if we convey that truth with love and back it with our own behavior.

Something we often forget is that it is not possible to preach one life and live another if we want our children to have a real understanding and acceptance of the principles we want them to have. We're reminded of a woman we know of who is openly involved with a married man on the one hand and is the mother of an eleven-year-old boy from a previous marriage on the other. She says she is deeply concerned about the television shows her son watches, and day to day, she monitors what he sees, and says she must often say no to him about certain programs. The sex and violence isn't good for him, she says. Her concern is something we may understand, but we can clearly see how hard it is for that boy to understand her at all, for what a different life he sees her leading, a completely opposite life-style from the principles she is apparently trying to instill in him. She's not kidding anyone but herself—certainly not a sensitive boy. Even an eleven-year-old can detect the difference, and the only "truth" he learns is the hypocrisy of grown-ups and a pattern of play-acting that will stay with him his whole life. How important it is for us to be sure that we *live* our truths as well as *speak* them, and when we speak them, that they are said with love and kindness.

. *Is it kind?* We women know how important kindness is, in our lives and others'. Kindness is our gift and our reward, in a world where our special and most unique gifts as women aren't rewarded with huge salaries, luxurious offices, or any of the other material benefits that may be visible to the world. We derive so much from words. We like to be noticed and complimented, we like building up. And if we like it, we should know that others do, too. There's no one better able to see the value of kind words than a woman, and no one better able to understand how far-reaching the effect can be.

Everybody can use a little building up, genuine and spontaneous, the kind that puts into the hearts of both the speaker and the recipient a really good feeling of well-being. Sometimes we can be a bit shy about expressing our thoughts to another person, afraid we'll be thought to be making meaningless compliments. Some women think we have so much inflated praise all around us on television or in newspapers and magazines, that *terrific* and *wonderful* and *sensational* are overused words these days. Not at all. How can we come out and tell a friend or stranger even how lovely she looks or how great he looks? Yet you know how important it is to you yourself to be affirmed in such a way. Everybody healthy in spirit tries to make themselves look as well as possible, and, by George, sometimes it takes a pretty long time, and you're going to love to hear it confirmed from someone that you look great. How about being that encouraging to someone else! We read a face that's telling us "I'm deeply unhappy," and maybe we can start a little green shoot of confidence and happiness by a real compliment. We all need those green shoots of happiness. You know that marvelous saying: "If you keep a green bough in your heart, the singing bird will come!" The husband who comes home defeated and discouraged needs to hear that he's a fantastic person as far as you're concerned . . . and that his enemies better shape up. The child who's struggling with a subject at school needs to hear from you that he or she's a great kid whom everybody in the neighborhood likes, and that when he or she has got that most important thing going for him or her, this deal can be conquered too.

Here's a story about a businessman, the president of a large corporation, who didn't lose the opportunity to say, "You're terrific," and changed two lives. The man was in his office discussing a business problem with one of the company's employees, an executive who had worked long and hard for the corporation for many years. The phone rang during their conversation, a call from the executive's wife. Before he took the call, the company president got on the phone to speak to the woman. "Before you talk to Bill," he said, "I just wanted to tell you what a fantastic man he is. We couldn't do without him here at the company. And I want to thank you, too. I know you've had to give up many hours with him so that he could do his job, but he's been essential to us all these years. I wanted you to know how much we appreciate him."

The company president didn't think again about this impulsive compliment. Then, a couple of days later, he received a call from Bill's wife. "I had to tell you what you've done for Bill and me," she said. "When I called the other day, it was to confirm an appointment to see our lawyers. We were going to start divorce proceedings. But when you spoke to me and told me how you felt about Bill and the company, I realized that I hadn't really seen him in that light for a good many years. It made me remember what a terrific person he is. So when we met that day to see the lawyer, I told him so. And we decided to try again with our marriage. Instead of going ahead with the divorce, we are buying a new home. Thank you. You're a terrific man, too."

The president was deeply moved by the call. As he was leaving the office that day, he happened to look at a sign that had been on his desk so long he'd stopped noticing it, but its sentiment had captured his spirit sure enough. The sign said: "Always be kind. Everybody's fighting a hard battle." Martha has shared this story over and over, for she was deeply touched by it.

*I set out immediately to inscribe that sentiment on a lovely piece of paper and place it conspicuously where Buckner and I both could see it every day, and maybe we could do some kind of good for someone, too. Wow, all of us need that kind of consideration—we all need kindness too, so I placed it right over our light switch just as we leave our room, praying it will keep ever before us that everyone's in a fray of some sort. I could never tell you what remarkable things happen when we all really go out of our way and try kindness . . . even when the person is difficult or looks totally self-contained . . . for all of us sometimes have tried to look the calmest when the storm was greatest.*

The company president never knew Bill was fighting a hard battle. He had never bothered to think that he might be. Bill was always so organized and businesslike, even while all those problems with his marriage were raging inside him, that the company president didn't calculate to be kind when his wife called. It was just a spontaneous feeling he had about Bill, some impulse that made him speak those few words about how really important Bill was to him. It taught the company president a lesson, and he's made a new and real effort to remember his friends', his family's, and his employees' hard battles and what a little kindness can do.

We never really know how we affect the people we speak to everyday of our life. Often we're so caught up in our own problems and chores that we forget to temper our words with kindness. We wonder how many women forget to say the nice things they think, right at home, to their husband and children. Living close to people day after day, it's easy not to bother, to forget that those familiar people are fighting hard battles, just as much as strangers. It's easy not to say something kind to those we take for granted. Martha remembers an occasion when Buckner was speaking to a large group and she was singing, something they've done many times together over the years. He's always gracious in complimenting her, but there was something special and unique about this, for this time, after the program, Buckner, very moved himself, said suddenly, "Martha, you've never sung better in your life, and what you sang tonight has never meant more to me." The compliment was so spontaneous and warm and touching that it brought tears: Buckner had heard the songs and hymns countless times before. It was just one of those moments. His words rewarded Martha for her efforts, and they meant so much more because they came from her husband. They were both touched and did not for a moment take the other for granted.

Communication in which we women take the lead tells us that we are loved, that we love, and that we care deeply about our family, that we see beyond the surface to the real person and know where our kindness can build up. Millie recalls a boy she dated way back in high school days who said, "I love you and if I ever change my mind, I'll tell you." Millie recoiled from that quickly and forever and she sees the unfortunate lives of some friends whose husbands must have that philosophy, for they seem never to hear the wonderful words *I love you*. Now, it's an empty kind of love that's never confirmed in words. We do need to verbalize our deep feelings and not take them for granted, or take it for granted others will know how we feel. Women are at ease in expressing abstract feelings and concepts. Emotions define their world, and they aren't afraid to speak them. That's a great gift, too, in a world so wanting to hear good things. And along with expressing feelings, we can spend a lot of time teaching our husband and our children to open up and express theirs if they aren't sensitive here. Some men actually are more sensitive it seems than their wives in this area—and those wives need to learn this gift from their husbands. A father who was greatly preoccupied with his work and had only limited time to spend with his children found that his nine-year-old son seemed increasingly alienated from him.

"I spend as much time as I can," he told his wife, "but I don't seem to reach him anymore."

"It's not the time," the boy's mother said, "it's that you treat him like one of your business associates. Just be kind to him, he's a little boy who needs to know you think he's wonderful."

The next time the man left on a business trip, he called his son from the office. "I just wanted to tell you that I think you are a terrific kid," he said.

The boy was embarrassed somewhat—and then

he said, very excitedly, "I'm not terrific, Dad. You are."

These few words were the start of a new kind of relationship. Dad had always thought his son was terrific. He just never mentioned it. And the little boy just never knew.

No matter how close a husband and wife are, neither of them is a mind reader. The joint effort and adventure that their life together represents needs to be confirmed all the time in both action and words. One of the most wonderful examples of communication between husband and wife is visible to all the members of Trinity Baptist Church. The man is both blind and deaf, and his wife is deaf. The church has a large number of deaf members and a special program of interpreters, so that every word spoken in a service, every song sung is interpreted in sign language from the front of the church. As Buckner speaks, his words are interpreted for the deaf. The man's wife then interprets every word into her husband's hand. When he "hears," it's through his wife. Their remarkable communication is a stunning example of the close bonds between them. Everything that comes to his mind from the world comes through her; he has no way of interpreting her actions or facial expressions. She must constantly tell him exactly what is being said, what she is thinking, what is happening.

"The Lord knew I was going to need my precious wife," he once said. "And I knew I needed her and we loved and needed each other when we married, for we shared our deafness, but I never realized at the beginning that I would need her the way I do now. God knew. For I've only been without my sight for a few years, and she's God's gift to me!" She is responsible for giving him bad news as well as good, and she has to do a lot of building up to enable him to get through his difficult, but extremely productive life, for he is an active, creative research assistant, very valuable to a large foundation. They both believe each to be God's gift to the other—you can see this so clearly.

The gift of communication, which we ought to treasure and use, has so many benefits, and we see the results at unexpected moments. Suddenly we encounter a situation that has unbelievable power and beauty. Martha tells about one such experience that happened to her and taught her an incredible lesson about what communication means. Trinity Baptist Church has many services and activities. Besides the department that serves the needs of the many deaf church members, there is also a home for neglected children, young boys and girls whose parents have mistreated them or cannot provide them with good homes. Many of these children, before coming into this loving relationship, have spent their entire short life with no affection, no kind words, no building up. In fact, many of their situations are enough to break the spirit or so it would seem.

Margie was close to fifteen when Martha met her—she asked shyly at a get-together for some pointers on how to do her hair and nails. Margie had never had any caring from her mother; it was hard to believe from her story of neglect and abuse that she could have gone through so much and still survived. A great example of the resiliency of the human spirit! She had survived, but she felt pretty bad about herself, it was clear, and she desperately needed friendship and love.

One Sunday evening, after a busy and exhausting day, Martha was thinking of staying home from the evening service to rest. Then she felt impressed to go even though she was very tired. Later she "knew" why this conviction to go was so strong. Margie rushed up to her at church that night. She had set her hair or done her nails, something she wanted to show off to someone who might be counted on to compliment her. It was easy to tell from her tone, if not her words, that she needed someone, and that she wanted to sit beside Martha in church.

Martha was delighted at this girl's trust, which she was honored by, so she encouraged Margie to sit with her. They slipped into the nearest pew, which happened to be the section reserved for the deaf down front facing the interpreter. Margie was so happy and looked so cute with her new hair-style that she behaved like an ordinary, carefree teen-ager.

One of the most beautiful young women in the city happens to be a member of the church, and also happens to be deaf, so she was sitting only a few places away from Margie.

"She's so pretty," Margie leaned over to whisper. "I wish I could look like that. And she's deaf, isn't she?" And after a moment's thought: "I wish I could tell her how pretty she is."

"You can. I'll show you how. You point, and then you make a circle around your face like this . . . that means in sign language, 'You're beautiful!' "

Margie leaned forward and caught the young woman's eye. "You're beautiful," she said in sign language.

The young woman's face lit up, and she smiled. Then she pointed at Margie and made a circle around her face: "You're beautiful, too," she said, and the joy in little Margie's face was truly beautiful to see. The spontaneous compliment from an unknown person had fixed Margie in the world that most of us know, where there are good and kind people. For a short moment, a few kind words, silent though they were, took her away from the loneliness and neglect that she'd known her whole life. And Martha experienced a moment of warmth, a "happening" powerful indeed:

*An experience like that takes tiredness away in an instant, and inspires a silent prayer of thanks for being allowed to share the moment, the communication without words between two people handicapped in their separate ways . . . yet certainly not handicapped when it came to sharing their feelings!*

The power of communication, truth, necessity, and kindness all give us wonderful opportunities to encourage and teach those we love and those we may never know. We can teach so many of the truths we believe in, we can touch hearts and minds with the words we women use so freely . . . that we "know" so well.

"You're beautiful" is something we can say about almost everyone, if we will, for everybody is beautiful in his or her own way. And by saying so, we might very well be able to change a life . . . perhaps even our own!

# Nine

# All You See Is Not All There Is

We remember seeing an episode of *All in the Family* a while ago, where Edith was being berated by Gloria for being downtrodden all these years by Archie. Edith responded with a line that spoke pages about what any marriage is: "Gloria, has it *ever* occurred to you that all you see is not all there is."

Poor Edith, the television-viewing world has often thought over the many years the show appeared. But Edith reminds us that there are areas of contentment in marriage that don't necessarily show up on the surface; there are rewards within that no one should be too quick to deny.

Contentment needs to be understood anew nowadays, especially if we're talking about women. Contentment to some people suggests complacency,

133

status quo, a lack of ambition to make things happen. To some, it even hints at hypocrisy, a word to cover up seething discontent that must be there. If a woman calls herself content, she must be kidding herself and everyone else, says the cynic. How can a wife and mother be content, when there are so many other things she could be doing? How can she be content, when the world of women has always been one of facing many and varied changes, in circumstances, in our bodies, in our status, even in the size of the circle of loved ones around us?

Yet there are many women who honestly consider themselves content, even lucky. They may find themselves in all kinds of circumstances; often it's a very ordinary life, running a household, raising a family, caring for and loving a husband, who is a partner in their contentment. They take their jobs seriously, they have very strong identities as women, they've learned to meet whatever life hands them with the best will and in the way that's best for them and their loved ones.

Such women aren't often heard from, but they live their life in a remarkable fashion: "I have learned in whatsoever state I'm in, therewith to be content" or in other words, "I'll bloom where I'm planted!" The *kind* of state is never predictable nor even the point here, nor is there any promise that every state in which one finds oneself would be happy or constant or without turmoil. No one knows better than women how quickly things can change, for better or for worse. So often, those changes affect the basic quality of our life—our deepest feelings—of love and fear and worry and responsibility. With the loss or gain of affection, honor or pride. We join in as our husband and children face the same losses and gains, but men, and the young, so often see achievements and defeats in terms of the concrete; we see the spirit behind them—those intangibles.

The real life of a woman is bound up with all the emotions from ecstasy to heartache in her pilgrimage—her long walk. There is an instinctive knowledge we have that often tells us how to act. No matter, really, whether it is biology or social conditioning that speaks to us; perhaps it is a combination of both. What matters is that we know some things instinctively. Sometimes we are able to create contentment out of circumstances that most women wouldn't find comfortable. Some women, for example, never marry. And of those there are some who live in bitterness and resentment their whole life. Yet others take the condition of being alone and find the best in it . . . and really bloom where they are planted. They find contentment in their work or in service, yet they are not "unfeminine." Again, it's our attitude toward the situation—married or single—that colors or drabs it. The deep instincts that all of us share as women enable us to see and understand what women have *always* known: that we can build our life and live it out beautifully in many ways if we are first and foremost comfortable with the fact of being women! For a woman who doesn't like being a woman in the first place has little chance at contentment.

A rising and ambitious young woman politician, well known for her controversial feminist beliefs chose not to run again immediately for office. Her seriously ill mother required care that was affordable only if the young woman put aside her political plans. Some of her colleagues saw it as a betrayal of what she stood for as a "feminist." A man wouldn't have given up his career, they thought.

"We women still have our different roles," she said. "True, a man might have not made this particular decision. I don't know. I made mine because it was right for me." Her instinct was profeminine—maybe not profeminist.

We know men who *have* changed every part of their life-style for their wife or family, so it's not fair or healthy for women to generalize about men either. We both know valiant men who are exemplary in their unselfishness about their own personal goals. One is a man whose wife left him with five children to raise and support because she wanted out. Let's hear it for him! He's doing a great job! Another is one of the most unselfish men we know, who because of his wife's lingering incurable illness had to remove himself from his first-choice profession and get into another type of work to accommodate her needs. We know others too—more and more. We women mustn't sell out to a harsh attitude. It does not become us one little bit.

Another young woman said, "I took my oral examination for my Ph.D. degree when I was eight months pregnant with my second child. I knew when the baby was born, I'd have other priorities, although at some time in the future, I'd be doing something I enjoyed with my education. Right now, I'm completely content being a mother. It's important for me. Other things will be important later."

It's gratifying to hear contented women speak of their life. But there are millions of women who lead what might be called ordinary lives and are not content. Many marriages are filled with friction and unhappiness. These women know that they are looking for contentment, but it seems to elude them. They try being inert intellectually and in every other way, they try allowing themselves to be totally dominated by their husbands, but this role brings them no sense of worth at all. In many cases it only intensifies the problem. There is a sense in which the quality of endurance is part of the nature of the spiritual woman. She endures in her marriage, as long as is possible to summon strength, even if it is unhappy, with the hope that God can use her graciousness and love to affect the lives of those around her, particularly the husband who might not share her spiritual framework and moral values. She can find contentment in the knowledge that while she cannot see the whole game or understand God's whole plan, she has a real part in it . . . and if her endurance is not used to foster a martyr's role, and she's really ready to face the situation squarely and perhaps do her own share of changing too, well, miracles still happen . . . over and over.

Yet Christian endurance has been much distorted of late. It doesn't mean that for the sake of a false peace and sham contentment a woman lays down her life and even her body to a tyrant. There is a point beyond which Jesus said a person need not go. When a husband (or wife either) is unfaithful, we believe the point has been reached. Here people begin splitting theological hairs. Where does unfaithfulness start? When a man or woman actually jumps into bed with another partner? Or does unfaithfulness start when a person departs in his spirit from the marriage contract? Now we're getting somewhere, for Jesus indicated that the basis of love and faithfulness was "attitudinal" not "glandular." He placed the emphasis of our faithfulness—both men's and women's—as well as our unfaithfulness within our hearts. That's where it all begins, according to Him who created us. He knows His creation, He knows. We do believe strongly, too, that when a man has fallen in love with violence, and his wife and children are the victims, he has broken the contract. A woman cannot then say, "I will be content." She can put aside her endurance and seek elsewhere for the peace her marriage fails to give her. Her children deserve that. Divorce is a sad decision, but there are times when it is the only possible one. Tragic but true.

Is there any way we can take out insurance, so to speak, for a good marriage, something that will give us the right climate for contentment to grow? There is, but it is something we *begin* our marriages with. This word *begin* is vital here, for marriage insurance, like airline insurance, is not easily obtained as the plane starts plummeting down. This "something" that we are to begin our marriage with is, at the very least, something that we must teach our children. The Bible asks a simple question that is, we believe, the most fundamental part of marriage. It applies to persons of every faith. It's something that should be answered by every man and woman who marries: "How can they walk together, unless they be agreed?" Unless a woman and a man agree spiritually, they cannot walk together in contentment. There are too many problems to face, too many questions whose answers are derived spiritually. Real spirituality can't in your wildest imagination be feigned in those desperate situations you will face together. You may rock along a little while, but you'll *not* escape the need for spiritual help—that inevitable need and yearning for God and His guidance. As Bishop Fulton Sheen so wisely has said: "It takes three to marry. You, your husband, and God."

That's a workable, logical ideal. How much more productive it is to start with that agreement than it is to spend a lifetime working to arrive there. Too often young couples don't consider the vertical relationship to God when they marry. It's totally horizontal in every sense. Today more than ever, people believe that romantic love conquers all, and when they reach the first chughole in love's little path, they discover that sexual love doesn't make it go away. Without that spiritual agreement, they have nothing with which to bridge their marriage.

The woman who finds herself in a marriage that lacks the necessary spiritual agreement is not likely to be content. There is no easy solution. She must be honest and come to terms with the fact that she disregarded the commandment of God that said that she and her husband must walk together in agreement, and accept the consequences. There's a kind of redemption built into that very attitude—it's a new beginning. But she must also know that God cannot be manipulated into reversing what has occurred. Yet a spiritual woman turns back again to love and its mighty power. It can oftentimes influence spiritual agreement, it can set right when started off wrong . . . it really can! Her spiritual presence in the marriage may change their lives. That knowledge may be the beginning of contentment. There is enormous hope when anyone in a marriage, either husband or wife, begins for the first time or even once again a spiritual walk.

It seems to us that the increasing divorce rate has a lot to do with the many marriages made between two people who did not walk together from the start. They shared no common spiritual framework; they agreed on no fundamental principles. We know this is not the only reason, but for women in such marriages, there comes a time often when they can no longer find contentment in their state, and the marriage is ended. But divorce alone is not going to give back what was missing. For every divorce, there is a woman left alone, if only temporarily, an unattached person in a society that doesn't feel quite comfortable with unattached women. Or maybe the women don't feel comfortable—or both; but that uncomfortableness is a fact, a very real life-style for many women.

In fact, the state of being left alone is particularly difficult for women, and it's something we see often. We know that women have a longer life span than men; it's almost a guarantee that a large percentage of older women will be widowed and spend their later years alone. Some women see their children, to whom they have devoted their life and energy, grow up and leave home. If those children have taken absolutely first place in her attention and affection, she pays a big price indeed, for the husband sitting across the way in a now-empty house may be almost a stranger. And what could have been wonderfully creative years for her can unfortunately turn into the saddest of lonely times. Two strangers sharing quarters. It's as if these women, too, are utterly alone . . . and that really should have been thought about early in marriage. In fact, it's never too late for a woman to avoid this situation by turning her attention to this very real world, knowing her children will leave the nest one day—and knowing that that's what's supposed to happen. She needs to keep her husband's and her life together loving, warm, affirming, vital, real, and fun (strangely enough, children themselves want and flourish in this kind of atmosphere and learn themselves how to be good husbands and wives). She should anticipate her future with great excitement as days of real personal creativity. And in this life, there are tragedies, accidents, illnesses that leave us alone and grieving. How can we find contentment in this lonely state?

We think that because most women have a natural "nesting instinct," they will agree that women are somewhat better at just plain survival than men; there's an inner structure of strength that's made up of knowing how to get through a day, a week, a year. We can keep on cooking and cleaning and doing chores automatically and give our lives the form in which our grief or aloneness may be contained and our loneliness held at bay. Being alone is not the same as being lonely. Loneliness can occur in a crowd. We have absorbed from our early training and the place women have in society the basic necessities of keeping life together. If we are nurturers and caretakers of our families, we are certainly that for ourselves. We may not all be trained to a career in the outside world, but we are all trained to survival . . . and that's no small gift!

But mere survival isn't contentment. Contentment is something that fills out our life and *is* what's real and warm to us. We think that women are attuned to finding contentment, because that is usually our real goal, not power or money, although we sometimes mistakenly believe those are what define or will bring contentment. But money and power should be seen for what they are—*just* satisfactions or gratifications or means to an end, not deep-down contentment. We realize it's not that simple, because many of the powerful and rich are *still* looking for contentment and freely admit this fact. What defines contentment is the full use of all our qualities as women, in good times and bad, in the wonderful, ever-changing, exciting relationship with human beings—with our husbands and children, with ourselves—and with the Lord. If we are fully alive to our opportunities in this world, it doesn't matter what state we find ourselves in, for there can be contentment . . . contentment that's possible.

We can imagine women in the throes of deepest grief and despair reading these words and saying, "You're wrong, there's no contentment for me. You have happy lives, with no problems, no loss that you are suffering through. It's easy to see the bright side, when the bright side is right in front of you. Don't talk to me about contentment when I have lost what was dearest to me." Well, first of all, we all feel when we're going through tough times that no one has ever been there before, that no one else has ever sailed in rough waters. That underlines our title: "All You See Is Not All There Is."

We can and we will talk about contentment. If it has been lost, it can be found again, because we believe that a woman's inner strength is fighting always to reach it. In our world today, it's terribly easy to substitute alcohol or pills for contentment, to run after empty goals and gratifications, and to be confused by promises that beckon to us from all sides. There are many tempting detours and byways on the long walk, but the promise of our pilgrimage is the promise that the Lord through His Holy Spirit is with us, and that His resources are always available to us.

It is true that as we write, we are contented women, but we are not women who have never had a problem. We have passed through grief and adversity, no more perhaps, but certainly no less than any woman. We have endured deaths of loved ones, occasions when the life of our spouse seemed to hang on a thread, when our many demanding responsibilities tired us out tremendously; we have borne children who've made it into this world healthy and happy and we've borne babies who didn't make it at all; we have been pushed to achievement in challenging roles that weren't predictable, roles that weren't and aren't simply defined, and very often, we have been confronted by situations demanding all the courage we could muster. We have been prey to jealousies, and the anguish they cause, we have sometimes lost sight of our own priorities, we have known confidence and the lack of it, we have been happy and unhappy at times—just like anyone else. In short, we have been ordinary women, subject to the ordinary experiences that befall every one of us . . . we have normal lives.

But we have also tasted all the joys that ordinary women are privileged to experience: We have loving husbands, we have wonderful children, we have happy homes. We have many satisfactions earned outside the home as well. We have contentment, and it arises, we believe, from our gratified acceptance of our roles as women and from our framework of faith that gives our lives meaning and allows us to tap the hidden resources of the Spirit, to find our contentment.

There is a story about a man who lived his whole life in poverty in the middle of a bleak, lonely sheep pasture in Texas. He never developed the land, he never allowed geologists to do surveys of his mineral resources, which is commonly done in parts of Texas. Finally he sold the land and the new owners called in the geologists who found that under that miserable field was one of the largest oil discoveries in the history of Texas. Millions of dollars a day began to flow from those hidden resources. The old man who had spent his life there never knew what his resources were. If he had made the effort, drawn on them, he could have been a part of royalty. In just the same way, we are part of the spiritual kingdom with infinite resources. As the wonderful song says: "I'm a child of the King!" We can choose to go on living on the surface in spiritual poverty and loneliness or we can dig deep, to discover the riches within ourselves and in the Lord. It's our choice. His promise that greater things will be seen and accomplished wasn't an empty one. When we fail as Christians or come up short as human beings, it's because we haven't really asked that His mysteries be shown us. When we give up our striving for contentment without a whimper, we haven't really tried to find it. We have to want it . . . *really* want it.

Martha's friend Vera is a longtime member of Trinity Baptist Church. Hers is the kind of story that scarcely seems to typify contentment, because everything about it seems to work against it. She lives alone, except for her two children, both of whom were stricken with muscular dystrophy as they reached their teen-age years. Vera's son Rahuell was stricken first and confined to a wheelchair; later his younger sister Thelma began to show similar symptoms. As the disease progressed, the children's father, already despairing over his son, reached the end of his tolerance and took out his helpless anger and frustration on his wife, Vera, and the children. He simply couldn't handle the situation.

There was no contentment for Vera, certainly, caught as she was between her husband and her children. She could see the long road ahead: Both children would need constant care and attention, they would need love. Would their father be able to give it to them? Or was it going to be a lonely walk for Vera?

Vera made a courageous and difficult decision.

She told her husband, when his frustration became unbearable that he could find another wife if he chose, but the children could never find another mother, and they could not endure his treatment. So she was alone, with no money, but with a talent for dressmaking that was close to artistry, and her faith. For years the three of them have been together, with Vera's son earning a degree from Trinity University, and her daughter finishing San Antonio College. They come to church each Sunday and sit down front, with the young man and woman in their wheelchairs in the aisle. Vera is much loved by all who know her; she is content and so very real, and if you ask, "How are you today?" she's likely to answer, "I don't know, let me think." No one can ever accuse her of pretending that she doesn't have times when she is feeling really down. But she has survived, with a lot of good humor and spiritual strength—and a remarkable son and daughter who represent courage in its finest sense. You have only to meet her and her children once to know that she has balanced the difficulties of her life with contentment—and so have they. She has coped well. Martha says her visits to Vera and her beautiful daughter and handsome son are joyful happenings:

*We do have lots of fun because we really love each other and relax in each other's company. One day I arrived when a woman had just left their home in a hurry. She had brought some clothes to be altered, and seeing the wheelchairs, etc., was terrified about what was "wrong" with them. Vera gently explained about muscular dystrophy and when her children had developed this disease. The woman had put her hand over her mouth and gasped, "Is it catching?" They tried to reassure her that it wasn't, but she left hur-*

*riedly anyway. Then Thelma told me with a real twin-*
*kle in her eye, "I'd rather have what I have than what*
*she has!" We laughed so heartily and hoped the lady*
*would see the light and come back.*

So Vera's decisions, many years ago, were moral and practical ones, and some that had to do with the intangible qualities of womanhood. Moral values aren't inflexible, but their range isn't very wide; we know what is right, even if it is difficult. If we act in a way that we know is not morally right, it's unlikely that we will be content in our lives in the world, or spiritually where we know ourselves best.

Few women face such clear and severe choices as Vera, and end up being alone because of duty and love. But so many women today do find themselves left alone. Divorce is a fact of our twentieth-century life, and the woman who is left by her husband, in spite of the millions in the same situation, is utterly alone and suffers all the grief and sense of loss that death causes . . . plus that enormous sense of guilt and rejection at the same time.

Suzanne's husband told her on their twelfth wedding anniversary that he was leaving her and their three children. "I had for some time sensed that things weren't right between us, but it was a terrible shock. The loneliness at home was unbearable, so I went back to work, and the first week was just awful. There were people around me, sure, but I hardly knew them and they certainly didn't care about my personal problems. But coming home Friday night at the end of the week was the worst. The house was empty, the kids had gone to stay with their father for the weekend. I was absolutely alone for the first time in twelve years.

"I had friends who'd said, 'Just call if you get to feeling down,' but you can't call people at six at night when they're getting dinner or sitting down with the family, and those are the times when you really feel alone."

It's hard to find contentment when you're suffering feelings of guilt and grief, anger and loneliness. You aren't home anymore where there is someone who is always on your side. We compete from the moment we set our feet outside the door, whether we are going to work or school or bridge parties. When we come home, we're supposed to be able to stop competing, we can be ourselves with people who care about us, who aren't competing with us.

Women who live alone don't have that. No matter how good and close our friends are, they aren't obliged to give that kind of constant support, the ear we need. "I miss my sweetheart," a widow in her seventies said sadly, and behind her words is an abyss of loneliness for which there is no instant cure. Wonderful memories help, but simply looking back is no solution.

Eventually, if we are to survive triumphantly, we must come to terms with our loneliness. We have to be able to say, "In whatever state I find myself, I will be content," and mean it. The initial shock of separation, for whatever reason, makes life almost unbearable. The grief we feel is overwhelming. And we're not going to say, "Well, you've been left alone, and you're grieving, but don't worry, it's OK." It's not OK; things are not going to be OK until you've lived through your time of grief. Grief has to be gone through; it's not erased in an instant. But the fantastic thing is, one day you look back, and you've gone through it. Time really is a great healer, and God has given us time. We can't reverse time and bring back what we've lost, but time can soften, take the edge off, make it possible once again to move ahead.

Accepting grief is something that we women know how to do. Like the abstract ideas of love, we deal in sorrow. We face real and serious situations and cope with them in practical ways. Grief is like a big wall that you have to wake up to and face every morning; you can't get around it, you can't leap over it, yet you have to get to the other side. We wait, then, we have patience if we are sensitive and wait for time to break down the insurmountable wall to a more manageable height . . . a surmountable wall.

Patience is so easy to talk about and so hard to put into action. It's the old problem of wanting and expecting instant solutions. We read a clever prayer—funny but true—"Lord, please give me patience, and I want it right now!" Overnight, we don't suddenly become a new person, though, by going out to meet new challenges, making new friends, not missing our husband and the family life we once had, not missing the contentment we had. But, with an effort of will and with time, it comes again. It does. We've said that Jesus never seemed to be in a hurry, but He got everything done. If He is our strength and our example, we can follow Him in His slow, steady footsteps . . . and be sure the path we walk He has walked once before—perfectly!

The woman left alone who has a strong spiritual framework, with a life whose hub includes the Lord, still has great comfort, even though time and tides take their toll, and she winds up with aloneness or whatever. The resources of the Holy Spirit are to be tapped and used. If a woman has a set of strong moral values, and faith, then God is always very, very near, and He is available to hear her when she prays—some things being such concerns she can hardly verbalize them. Jesus said He'd do that for us when we couldn't. He surely knew. The very fellowship of faith—the church—gives the lonely, grieving woman a foundation for contentment in her new circumstances . . . for she has a family once again!

Are there some other practical things that could be done to ease the pain? Patience alone gives us only time; what more can we do? When grief comes, as it does inevitably in situations of loss, Buckner and Martha counsel—be kind to yourself—for we are sometimes very tough on ourselves when we particularly need to be kind.

It's true that difficult situations, times of grief seem to stir up some form of masochism or self-pity from the depths of our being. We're going to make ourselves shape up, work harder, ignore it (when we certainly can't). We are going to put on a brave front, although everyone knows our heart is breaking, and we're not fooling anyone. Yet strangely enough we are extremely kind to another person who might be suffering in exactly the same way. It's tremendously helpful and quite sound to take our own advice, the advice we'd give to someone else to take it easy, let things slide for a while, don't rush to find the answers. Try it—step outside yourself and take your own advice as you would your best friend's—you need it, you deserve it. We might notice that a grieving friend looks tired, and say, "Take a nap; the world is going to go on while you rest." But in a similar situation, we look at ourselves in a mirror and see how tired we are, and we're determined to be brave, not to take our own advice, to prove that we can go on. Remember Scarlett O'Hara's words: "I'll think about that tomorrow!"

Then turn your mind down to slow motion. There's no need to cope with everything at once. There will be time later . . . and who knows but that in the waiting time we allow ourselves, things could focus better and softer.

We know that to someone in the middle of a great loss, we sound like the situation that occurred between Millie and Tyler the other day. Millie was applying some medicine to Tyler's scraped knee. She assured him that it would not hurt.

"How do you know?" Tyler replied. "It's not your knee!"

It's hard to give advice, because however many sad and tragic things we've been through, it's not the same as being in the midst of such a situation. But as a doctor's wife and a pastor's wife, we have shared in the lives of many women who have met and conquered their grief, the fact of being alone, and they have new contentment if they were determined and wanted to find it.

Sometimes having to go to work or even going to work when you don't have to has a strange benefit—it helps alleviate loneliness or the new experience of just being alone. We have a glowing tribute for a woman who found herself alone with a child to support. She is a remarkable woman, who had worked at a legal position in a prominent law office until she was seventy-six years old, more than forty years, retiring only because of a sudden change in her eyesight. She worked all those years supporting her daughter from the time she was ten years old, and was total mother and friend at the same time. Her spiritual strength taught the daughter so much and she understood God's love in Christ very early. The woman worked tirelessly for little pay, considering her important job as a legal conveyancer. She even gladly gave advice and her knowledge to judges on the bench who called upon her for her expertise. She did this year after year—at about one-third the pay that a man would have received. We know that and she knows it, too—and due thanks to the women's liberation movement, for in this area particularly we are very supportive of their efforts for equal pay for women. But to the honor of the company where she worked, they really believed in her and her abilities totally, and were undaunted by her age, encouraging her to stay long past the ordinary retirement age. They also had a good deal, but so did this woman—the value of her talents took precedence over manditory retirement. She was and is absolutely great! Her stability in every sense meant so much to her daughter, to whom she wrote just recently, "I've loved you since nine months before you were born!"

What a wonderful revelation that statement is, how revealing of the life of Billie Howell, and how meaningful for her daughter—Martha.

*I had been thinking of all she had given me inside as well as outside—and I wanted her to know how much I love her and appreciate her, so I shared the feelings with her once again in one of our long-distance calls not too long ago. She wrote me in response a wonderful letter, which concluded with those eloquent lines. A mother's copability is enormously important to her children—a gift really.*

So if you're alone and finding paths to contentment, remember you still have great gifts to give and you are giving them all along the way—that ought to be really encouraging. What a wonderful solution, really, for dissipating grief: getting out of yourself, refusing to wallow in your situation. Suffering can be very attractive for some women—you get more attention perhaps than you've ever gotten. And that's a strange magnetism. Attention takes away some of the loneliness temporarily. It's too easy to "enjoy" suffering when we're surrounded by people encouraging us to indulge ourselves, or when we're surrounded by sympathetic people. Grief may be necessary, but enjoying it is not. Women sometimes might not "feel" much like going out to work or doing any of the jobs work involves. But feeling like doing something often and mostly never has anything to do with the doing of worthwhile and necessary things. In fact, most of the really great things done in our world have been done and are being done by people who don't feel good. They have not succumbed to functioning on feelings alone. Waiting until you "feel" like doing something is a sloppy and lazy pattern—a very bad practice indeed—and it's bad for you. You can change that habit, and you must to really accomplish worthwhile things in this world. It's kind of like exercise. People say, "I don't like to exercise. It doesn't feel good." It does not have to feel good; it's preventive medicine. It's doing something that will play a part in the future and make it better.

That's how we deal with our losses and our grief. We must have the faith to believe in a bright future that is possible and not full of misery. It takes a lot of self-discipline to bring yourself to allow time to smooth out some of the sharp edges of suffering, and a lot of discipline to face being alone. But women have always known how to pull themselves together and go on. We do especially well when we realize that many of these solutions aren't "instant ones," and when we calmly and confidently trust the Lord and accept His pace, along with His peace. And like Millie with the bottle of medicine for Tyler's knee, we have to admit that it will hurt for a time, but the healing powers of time and the lord are resources we can always draw on to bring us back to contentment.

# Ten

# Be It Ever so Humble

Every time we hear people say that the home is disintegrating, that the family is out of style, and that motherhood is a dead-end job, we get a little annoyed. We know it's simply not true. We have the evidence of our own eyes—and our own experience—to prove them wrong. The home, motherhood, children, the fascinating mixture of all three are things we and multitudes of women still know and thrive on; it's not an easy job by any means, but so endlessly challenging and exciting, so meaningful and fulfilling.

### Martha: Motherhood Then—and Now

This was one of "those" mornings, when you think you've got it all together, and "it" has got you all apart! I had gotten up early, had already walked my three miles, gone to the store, gotten the kids off, fixed breakfast for two and lunch for one, and whew!—they were in school on time, it was *just* 8:30 A.M. My husband had left for the office, and I was relishing those thirty minutes between 8:30 and 9 o'clock for coffee, newspaper, orange juice, and even a little snooze if possible; *then* I had ten dozen other things to get done before noon. Then—the phone rang! Oh what a simple phone ring can do. I'm reminded of the old farmer who finally decided to get a phone after years of resisting. A friend was visiting him and the phone rang—and rang—and rang. The old farmer never moved to answer it, but kept talking calmly with his friend. "Why don't you answer it?" his friend asked, and the farmer said, "I only answer when *I* want to. I put that thing in for *my* convenience, not theirs!" I really admire a cool fellow like that, but I'm not made up to do that. Curiosity gets me to it on the first ring. When it rang during my precious thirty-minute interval, the voice on the other end said: "We're waiting for Lisa!" I tried to be cool, so I just asked one question: "Who are you?" Fair enough, huh? It was Lisa's orthodontist's *new* nurse, who couldn't quite understand how we'd forgotten an appointment made only six weeks before when we'd been given a slip of paper with the time on it. (Mercy, where was that paper? Don't ask me, I'm only the child's mother, her influence for being a great organizer—paper? I couldn't even remember seeing it at all!) She was nice, but felt Lisa must come, for no appointments were open in the forseeable future. I said calmly, "Surely, we'll get right over." (*Over* was twenty miles away!) What was I saying? This would be like preparing for the Battle of the Bulge. Calling the school, picking up Lisa, oh yes, getting on something besides a robe, which I had just gotten back into from the previous activities. But *certainly* we'll make it in—minus fifteen minutes. Well A. J. Foyt never set the record we did, plus he doesn't have to go by the school *before* the Indy 500. We made it, Lisa's teeth got tightened or something, and I sat in the car wondering about us modern-day mothers . . . hmmm. Then, at last, we were headed back for the school when Lisa gently and carefully, very carefully, shared something with me—she'd forgotten her lunch! Could we go back home a minute? Well, I smiled, why not? It's such a sad sight to see a grown woman cry in public. We got the lunch—my confidence in my organizational ability had had another setback—but I'd call the whole episode a lesson in humility I told myself, right? I needed to *understand* the disorganized of the world. Joke! No, really, it wasn't disorganization at all, just a rather typical morning of a typical modern mother—it was also 11:30. What's for lunch? And *where* is that little slip of paper with *all* those errands I must do before noon—oh, little slips of paper are for the birds! I'll do what I can—and if worry seems necessary—I'll do it "tomorrow"—if time permits!

I've thought of that experience often—and others like it. It was a teaching process much more powerful than any schoolroom: Lisa and I had learned a lot. She *requested* a bulletin board for all her little slips of paper, so she could be reminded of her future appointments; I shared with her over and over that "ordinarily" you shouldn't drive like A. J. Foyt on the expressways—it was really dangerous and oftentimes quite expensive; she and I worked out how she could remember her lunch; and I told her the importance of being flexible in this busy world. She and I sang a little funny duet in the car coming back and found out we can harmonize—and I took a look at my then-little eleven-year-old and saw beneath those braces the beautiful work of our most gifted orthodontist and the blossoming of a beautiful young lady! And little girls and mothers and forgotten slips of paper and everything had blended into a remarkable awareness of the privilege of the gift of a child, a gift that grows more beautiful as it's tenderly cherished!

Oh, that was *some* day and one most women—most mothers—*know* about, for all of us mothers lead surprisingly similar lives in the both charming and disarming world of children. We *do* have stars in our eyes when we think of motherhood. And rightfully so because it is undoubtedly the most demanding job in the world—whether you're good at it or not or whether you even know it or not. Mothers don't deal primarily with things like detergents and toothpaste and dishwashers and hair spray as TV commercials would make you think. Mothers deal in human beings. And everything they do in every way affects the gray matter and spiritual and emotional makeup of their children. Mothers who realize this or mothers who don't *still* can't escape this. When you have children, you're a mother every moment of your life—either good, bad, or indifferent. You don't decide that you'll "mother" today and take off tomorrow or that you'll influence your children for good today or you'll plan your influencing strategy for tomorrow; you're influencing all the time—for excellence or mediocrity. Your attitude speaks so loudly, your children hear even your silences. Are you convinced now about this responsibility? It's not a job—it's a life, and it's terrific!

I got to thinking about how different mothers' roles (and maybe rolls!) are today from the mothers of yesteryear. And if we don't keep our thinking straight here, we're liable to think she did a better job—with her seemingly unlimited time of rocking on the front porch, shelling peas, knowing at breakfast what dinner would be, taking her afternoon bath and being spruced up at four to have dinner ready by five or six (certainly not a moment later!), plus washing and ironing the laborious "old" way, and really making rolls quite differently (not having the joy of seeing that little doughboy jump out on the counter after having whacked the package!), patiently darning socks (my daughter would think I was cussing if I said darning anything), listening to the radio, going to bed quite early, and getting back up again to do it all the same way the next day. Horrors! Have we modern mothers gone down the drain? Not on your life! Some days I would cherish a routine like that (not many in a row, however), but our contemporary life-style has to be seen for what it is. A mother today lives in a totally mobile society (where she is the primary chauffeur), in a highly interpersonal, socially changing society (which she needs to be able to interpret to her children), and in a terribly needy moral climate (which demands her best ideas and active efforts to try to keep it on some kind of moral track for her children's welfare). In other words, a mother today lives in a world so challenging and so needful of her best efforts, that aloofness and uninvolvement are hardly options at all. It's a world that's a "whipper snapper" to handle—and a majestic opportunity at the same time! Why some of our pioneer foremothers would run for shelter to the "hard life" of those days in the past if they had to face even one day of some of the pressures of mothers today. I'm surely not belittling or showing less than full gratitude and respect for their devotion in a terrifically difficult set of circumstances, but I think it's time we quit glorifying the past and put some glory in the present. Are we afraid of this? We shouldn't be. This respectful understanding of our own many responsibilities should oil the gears of our varied efforts and activities with confidence and courage and give us the feeling that our modern-day "wagon train" and "Indian fight" might even be somewhat more complicated. In other words, we learn and gain courage from our valiant mothers of the past, adjust and live courageously in the present, so our offspring will do thusly in the future. A casual thing?—or everything!

What mother has not had some day, and probably many, similar to the following:

*The early morning car pool . . .*

*A PTA Committee Meeting on how to handle the narcotics problem in junior school, how to help a child whose home seems to be falling apart, what to do about the problem of a teacher who can't seem to relate to her students (sad, but true sometimes), other various problems within the school where your ideas are requested and needed . . .*

*An appointment at the orthodontist for one child at 3 P.M., the pediatrician at 4 o'clock for another (doctors used to be able to come to the home, remember?) . . .*

*Somewhere in the day at least making things manageable at home, figuring the whats, hows, and whens of dinner, such as when to eat between your husband's late appointment and your son's baseball practice and your daughter's after school skating party . . .*

*Then trying to look and be halfway decent so you can really be the kind of delightful companion your husband desires and deserves . . .*

*Remembering of course that everybody's had a hard day and they look to you whether you're ready or not for lots of listening time and understanding time and counseling time . . .*

*And then usually falling to sleep quite late to wake up to a completely different kind of day the next day. No boredom here—really a challenge to keep priorities straight and your family's needs first and your disposition at its best for them! Not simple at all. This challenge every mother still knows is hers.*

Part of the tired feeling of the modern mother, I think, stems from some sort of guilt she experiences way down deep that she can't live both life-styles at the same time—the pioneer woman and the modern household executive. One life looked more difficult because it lacked so many modern conveniences, when in effect, it was probably simpler in the area of emotional stress and healthier in the physical sense. Women's roles then were plain and limited and even required them to stay within certain boundaries. They did not have nearly so many voices of instructions shouting at them to be here and do that and share in this and lead in that; in fact, they didn't even have the transportation to leave home! So having fewer major decisions to make does take the stress out—and the challenge too, one might say. But, of course, their lives were hard in their own way and we know that no mothering is done either then or now as a "free ride." So the guilt should go about doing things the old way. Why should I boil my clothes in the backyard when I have a washing machine and can wash my clothes and be a parent-helper in my child's schoolroom in the same length of time. My interest in my child and his knowledge of this should impress him surely as much as the fond remembrance of mother boiling the clothes in the backyard. Or why should I feel that delicious cookies carefully selected and bought for a school party are not bought with the same love that I could have "made" them with if my husband and I had not had the joy of and taken the time for a private luncheon together that same day, strengthening our ties and love. Priorities are primary! There's no room for guilt when you're rightfully placing people above things and household procedures and food preparation and all sorts of demands. People and relationships are first—and if by "boiling clothes," so to speak, everyone is edified and impressed—great! But it won't happen today—don't expect it. They want *you* and your time and interest in them. And with all of our modern conveniences—if they free us to be this kind of person and if we really make these modern conveniences work for *us*, then the more of them the merrier! Right on, GE and Westinghouse and Whirlpool and all the rest!

## Millie: The Vitality of Self-Discipline

Usually at some point in my lectures to high school students—and often other type audiences as well—I mention that I feel there is an attitude being propagated lately that is destroying the integrity of our young people in America. It is expressed in a bumper sticker I have seen on many cars stating, "If it feels good do it." In my opinion this is encouraging a complete lack of self-discipline and irresponsibility in the American people.

In other words, if something feels good to you, do it, regardless of the repercussions it may have. Let me state early that this topic can be approached from two directions. I began with the negative approach first. Obviously, if we have no self-discipline in our life and operate only on a feeling level we are not much above animals. Self-discipline, I feel, is the key to getting the most and best out of life and it affects all the areas of life really, taken in this order.

The results of self-discipline or the lack of it in our physical lives are obvious. If we let ourselves over-eat and become too fat a whole series of medical problems becomes more likely—hypertension, diabetes, depression, heart disease, and so forth. It is well established in documented data that exercise and proper diet can control or perhaps in some cases prevent some of these problems. However, if we do not want to discipline ourselves to exercise because it is uncomfortable at first or diet because it does not feel good to be slightly hungry, then we are going to pay the price.

I think one of the most important factors that determine whether an individual has a happy, productive, fulfilled life is whether or not he has self-discipline. It is the ingredient that makes all the difference in the world as to the quality of life. It is like salt in many respects. How tasteless most of our food would be without salt. Just a sprinkle of it can change a tasteless dish into a delicious one and what a difference a sprinkle or two of self-discipline can do for changing our lives from dull, drab ones to radiant and abundant ones.

Everyone has pity for the individual who cannot discipline himself in regard to food and becomes grossly overweight. Or the individual who cannot control his drinking and becomes an alcoholic. Or who lets his body deteriorate from lack of exercise and reaps all of the degenerative diseases that accompany that condition. But far too many Americans fit into this category simply because they have no self-discipline in their life. Why don't they? Because too many practice the philosophy of only doing things that feel sensually good to them. In other words, if it feels good, do it. If not, forget it.

What a price they pay in the end for this type of thinking and living. Ken sees many patients who are the end product of this type of living, and they are sad. Fortunately they are in the minority. Most of his patients are individuals who have practiced self-discipline most of their life or at least are now practicing it. And how different the life of the self-disciplined is compared to the former individuals mentioned.

I have mentioned some of the negative results of this type of philosophy, but looked at from another approach it can have great merit. Some very good things feel good, too.

First, let's look at discipline regarding your physical body. Nothing feels better than a highly conditioned body, one that is receiving regular exercise and proper diet and rest. These things don't just occur without awareness and discipline. I have written an entire book, *Aerobics for Women,* extolling the benefits of regular exercise and throughout the book the key word is *discipline*—sticking with it even when it doesn't feel good because the good feeling does come eventually.

To grow in our spiritual life also requires discipline. Reading the Bible daily nourishes our spiritual life just like food does the physical body. To me the result of discipline in every area of our life brings feelings of self-satisfaction and pride, and many fringe benefits.

In our very up-to-date, with-it, modern society you would think preaching this type of doctrine or thinking would be close to heresy, but I have not found this to be true. At least not with the majority of young people I have come in contact with. I firmly believe kids want and appreciate your total honesty in "telling it like it is." I also believe they want guidelines to live by and for someone to say this is still right and this is still wrong. And many parents who say, "I don't tell my children what to do because I don't want to inhibit them. I want them to feel free to do their own thing," I feel are simply "copping out." It takes time to sit down with your children and explain or discuss with them moral principles, and many parents simply do not want to take this time away from what they would rather be doing for themselves. It is much easier for them to say, "Do what you think is best." And unfortunately in many cases that turns out to be whatever their friends or peer groups are doing, and not always what's best for them.

Self-control, like self-discipline to me represents the good life not only for me but for those I love.

## Martha: A Dirty Place to Play

People are funny about their homes. Really funny. Some take very little interest, some *some*, and others place almost too much emphasis on the house rather than the home. There are houses you like to "view," not visit; have tea in, not spend time in; houses that reflect decor, not depth—oh, all sorts. When you find decor and warmth all at once, you have an elegance of spirit and your house has turned into home. A magical thing! "Things" in a house don't guarantee warmth or even beauty; the intangible spirit of a place is IT. You can, if you're financially able, even buy a store window complete with all the perfect combinations of interior decor, yet it shall remain totally sterile without people and joys and noise and fun and talk and problem solving and relating—that's *home*.

Now, I love beautiful decor—in fact, making things beautiful with plants, color, art, elegant material, comfortable furniture, all is an art in itself, and fun; every home should have beautiful things. Good taste, however, is not dependent upon money; if not innate it can be learned. Children ought to be surrounded by beauty—no doubt about it. And by meaningful things that have been lovingly passed down from generation to generation. And things that represent experiences you've all had, places you've all been, things you've done *together.* We have lots and lots of things that speak to us of other times, other life-styles, of days gone by, and of marvelous enriching experiences we've shared in various parts of the world. These things speak and inspire and give a sense of continuity to life—like that very prized little handcarved ivory ring made by a great, great uncle during the Civil War while he was sitting around a campfire before the Battle of Bull Run. He shared in a letter the feeling of a soldier who was tired and trying to take a piece of ivory and make something beautiful in an ugly situation. He wrapped this little ring in that letter and it was carefully loved and cared for all these past years since he died the very next day at Bull Run. Something beautiful out of something bad— that little ring speaks to us. Or the painting I'm looking at at this very moment done at Montmartre in Paris—a picture of the very umbrella table where our children (then ages fifteen, twelve, and six) and my husband and I sat and ate and felt a part of the big world beyond our own backyard. We would see the great art of the world and we would learn of the steadfastness of great things, and we'd talk under that umbrella that I'm looking at, so we bought the painting of that scene—not a practical way to spend money you say? I reply, quote me a price for adventure and a loving glimpse of this big old world and wide-eyed children who will travel it often and hopefully want to caress it with their own great contributions to it; quote me a price even for the symbol of it all—that painting is priceless now. Or the little, crudely made wooden plaque on the wall given to me after singing in the church in Warsaw, Poland, by the pastor, a man whose hand I grasped to capture his spirit and strength, a man who had served his people for forty years—through Hitler's rampage to Russia's domination. Who had had to live in the woods during World War II in a secret place and whose God-given courage and ministry through everything had seen him and his people through it all. Lots of us had known of him by reputation. I was astonished at his gift—handmade—upon which are written words of encouragement and a Scripture about singing. That speaks to us all, its value is in its spirit—and that's what home is all about.

The best decor, regardless of style, is everything that gets not in the way of but encourages real life experiences and wonderful reminiscences; all children need these things. So a house *does* contain things and should, but it's a home when these things are the servants of the inhabitants.

Now that's all good and well, but to face reality, every woman has always known and *still* knows that there are a lot of menial tasks in keeping a home lovely, functioning, and warm all at the same time. Nothing easy about this—and there's a problem inherent here if we don't watch it. That is the problem of how to keep house without losing home. That's not so simple. In the everyday tasks that present themselves so unwelcome like dirty dishes, dust, spills, smears, broken things, unmade beds—oh, you know it all—those "character-building" jobs sometimes scream louder than the kids. I say "character-building" because a friend of many years used to say that washing dishes or ironing, I think it was, or something like that, was so endless and so easily undone that it must be "character-building" only. We laughed and wished for more glamorous character-building mundane things. There are just some things that have to be done and they're for the birds. And anyone who *never* tires of them at all simply must have the least interesting pursuits in the world. So what to do? How do we get it done and keep house and home together?

The important thing is not the *way* you get the menial things done at home, but just that they are done. You may find you need outside help—that's OK, too. Getting it done is the important thing while keeping intact you and all your human relations within your home!

We all know women who feel guilty that their floors don't shine as brightly as somebody else's. Mercy! If you want to feel guilty (heaven forbid!) they're so many more important things than that to feel guilty about—and even rightfully so—such as the neglect of children and the neglect of involvement in social issues. Again, in the area of keeping house itself, managing well to get those menial things done *however* and keeping their importance in the proper perspective is *it*. To remember that they're not first though necessary and that they're not important enough to be all-consuming is vital. If "things" get the upper hand and make you crotchety and unpleasant, take hold and drop them for a while. They'll wait for you. *People* are more important. If I am making this attitude sound easy, like snapping your fingers, you're misreading. It's difficult, not only because we've been nurtured for generations to feel our housework equals our worth, but heavy, finger-pointing commercials (advertisements) today make you feel, if you're not on guard, that mother's greatest role is in the products she uses and that if she permits a ring around anything, she's down the proverbial drain! Have you watched how most of these superwomen on commercials act around their family? The father is really ridiculed for not knowing which drain opener to use, the daughter can't find the correct deodorant, and the kids do nothing that makes the mother smile more than falling down in a puddle so she can use her special detergent! I must have a different group around here—they couldn't care less about any of that and would laugh me into my rightful scorn if I placed such emphasis on such little things. We're interested in each other and in each other's interests and we do, in a healthy perspective I think, manage to stay clean, clothed, and well-groomed only as a means to the end! Often when they see some ludicrous commercial that makes everybody look like nincompoops, they'll say, "Please remember, don't buy that ever!" And I don't!

This is not written to say that getting things done, putting first things first, and relating well is simple at all. I used to be more of a perfectionist about the house, but that was too much of a burden to bear; too much was sacrificed like fun and relaxation and real enjoyment of the home. It could never look really perfect, so the obvious result to a perfectionist was to remain pretty upset quite often. In fact that's probably the reason for being a perfectionist anyway—so you can worry all the time because nothing is ever going to be perfect. Ridiculous! Fortunately, I saw through that and dropped as much of that highsounding trait as I could—still aiming at the highest and best, but not on puny things. I'm not saying that I had kept the house looking perfect, but I was upset if it wasn't—and upset if, when it did look perfect, somebody would mess it up. Let's face it, some women can't even leave a dirty place to play. Ah yes, a dirty place to play. How those five words spoke to me about twenty years ago. We had moved into our first home—all new and sparkly and fresh—and along with us in this new, sparkly, fresh home was a new, sparkly, peppy, never-stopping, ring-tailed tooter, lovable, curious, fantastic, one-year-old boy baby and world-beater: Mike. He was always on top of, underneath, inside of, and wrapped around everything. He was and still is a charmer, and his curious mind and determined ways have stood him in good stead—he's learned and accomplished more than lots of folks ever do, but those types of children in a totally spotless, nonflexible, perfectionist household don't mix. Something gives. That's all. Either some things are allowed to get out of place in the house to make way for a fun-loving little boy, or things get out of place in the boy, and he sees a house-loving mother instead of a home-loving one. Oh sure, there are kids who are little stinkers and really have to be disciplined a lot, but I'm not speaking of that—only the natural fun a child needs to be able to accomplish in his own home.

Well twenty years ago I had this combination and I read a remarkable story in *Parent's Magazine* about a mother who really was a superperfectionist housekeeper. She was not a homemaker, but thought she was. Her little son so dreaded her days of endless cleaning and "spit and polish" because she was so harsh with him in his normal boyish pursuits. He really saw her attitude and she shared with the readers how he taught her to relax and enjoy. One day she was laboring furiously toward her goal of spotlessness when a gentle tug was felt on her skirt. She looked into the face of a boy who felt second place in her affections that day: "Mommy, please save me a dirty place to play!" My! Call it what you will—our homes need to be "dirty places to play" or "comfortable places" or "warm spots" or whatever is conducive and tailor-made for really being ourselves and really feeling *at home!* The Lord knew I'd better learn this early, for two years later came another charming go-getter, Steve, and then six years after that, our wonderful daughter, Lisa, who would need to "catch on" to keeping both house and home for the rest of her life! A woman is never finished learning—Lisa will never finish learning—and I haven't either. That's why it's challenging!

So any woman who really comes to grips with it knows that everything is relative, that a perfectly spotless dwelling is only good if it can comfortably allow a little child to play, for if it shuts him or her out, it's not just bad, it's evil. A beautifully groomed child is a delight only if someone has carefully helped her to be groomed inside with the finest of attributes, otherwise, it's exterior-ville all the way and probably for the rest of her life. A perfectly, gorgeously decorated house is glorious only if it's a real home! Otherwise it's like being in a parade of homes.

Sign: "Homes for Sale" is incorrect; houses are for sale, homes cost a lot more, for they are not bought but wrought out prayerfully, carefully, and thoughtfully with much interior work done on the inside—of the occupants!

So a home should never be taken for granted, for it is precious indeed. Isn't it strange and unfortunate how we do take our homes for granted sometimes, particularly if things are going well. We're peculiar that way. We seem not to realize what we've got, what a treasure, for often we even forget to thank God for such a place. Too often problems rather than joys get

171

our attention, stir our senses; way too much and too often we respond to negatives as though they required much more consideration. We need to quit this; it's wrong and can become a habit that ages and "cantankerizes" human beings so obviously that they find that having always cozied up with negatives only joins them with negative people and joys just can't crash their party. I've heard people say, "But that's 'reality'"—all these problems. Well, so are the good things *real*—just as real—love, joy, peace, truth, goodness, faith, kindness, fun, gentleness, and all the others. They just need to be nurtured as carefully as we do the negatives. What a world this would be if we'd underline the joyful! If we'd cultivate the habit of *joyfulness!*

We human beings seem to notice our blessings and treasures only when they are absented from us. Ah, then we know what we've had, what power there was in the familiar. Let me share with you something I read a few weeks ago in the aftermath of an earthquake that devastated a town, a story that so touched me and still does—another "little boy's" lament. A little boy was found sitting in front of where his house used to be. He said so touchingly, "Home didn't seem like much till it wasn't there." He *said* it—he really did. How careless and casual we are with the essentials of our lives. Let's take a new look—a *good* one—and thank God in joy and—enjoy!

Every woman, when she seriously thinks of what she *still* knows, *still* knows the value and intrinsic treasure of her home, for it is truly her most tailor-made, comfortable, and natural habitat. She was born equipped to know more about this than any other creature!

Millie: Home Sweet Home—Why?

172

Home. What fantastic and wonderful memories that word can conjure up for many of us. Unfortunately for some, perhaps sad memories as well. But I know personally whenever I think of home I have a warm and happy feeling come over me. No matter how old I seem to get the feeling never changes. I grew up in what by today's standards might be called a deprived childhood at home because my family was not financially successful. We did not have much money or a big, elaborate home, but, my goodness, we had something far more important than lots of money—we had *love*. We all loved each other. Now that may sound trite and certainly nothing new, but it is an ingredient that is sadly lacking in many homes today. When I say we had love I mean by that that we truly cared for each other in a self-sacrificing manner. I was fortunate to have a grandmother who lived with us who taught me some wonderful things about life. She was a marvelous Christian woman who always had time to help others when they had a problem.

My mother had to work outside the home during part of my childhood, but, oh, what glorious times we all had when she and Daddy got home in the evening, as we shared dinner with my two sisters around a noisy, but happy kitchen table. I was discussing my childhood years with a friend the other day, as the subject had come up while we were talking about our own daughters and their desires to have countless numbers of slumber parties at a friend's home. I remarked that my mother always said yes when I asked her if I could spend the night with a friend because she knew, almost without a doubt, that I would probably go and be home by dark anyway. Because when evening came and I was away from home there was a terrible yearning inside me that came over me to go home. No matter if I was having a good time—I still would think about what a good time everyone was having at home and what good food my mother had prepared. Because to me she was the best cook in the whole world.

I have often tried, as an adult who has had many psychology courses, to define what it was that drew me so strongly home to my family at evening time. As I said, our home was simple, certainly no outstanding entertainment, not even a telephone for many years, but it had something great going for it and the only thing I can figure out that something was a common love in caring for each other.

I mentioned earlier that we loved each other in a self-sacrificing manner. One instance of this love shall always remain burned in my memory. I had been sick several days with a very bad case of measles. My eyes were swollen and I spent much of the day in a darkened room. Needless to say this was not a happy situation for a young, active child. My father wanted so much to cheer me up that he walked seven miles to the nearest large town (as we did not own a car at that time) to buy me a big, red, rubber ball with white stars on it, which took money from a budget that could not afford it. Just to cheer me up! That, folks, is love—*LOVE*. Something that all the money in the world can't buy.

I have seen examples where fathers provided their children with every material thing that their heart could desire and when the child grew up he couldn't care less about that parent. Never took the time to call, write, or even say I love you. But my father Thomas Clark who might not have been the biggest financial success in the world, won my love, gratitude, and undying loyalty with such acts of love as I just mentioned. Please don't misunderstand what I am trying to say. Many children who have received unlimited material blessings all their life do love their parents, but material provisions will not assure you of your child's love in return.

Every day of my life I understand more and more the full meaning of that little wall plaque you see in many homes that says, "Be it ever so humble, there's no place like home." There are those who stand and say the family is disintegrating and in the future will cease to exist—hogwash. God created the family and it will never cease to exist until the world does.

No matter how wretched the home may be that an individual comes from, there is still a bond that pulls him back to it and, of course, even a stronger bond if the individual was fortunate enough to have a happy home.

I can truly say my home was a "Home Sweet Home"—and I think I know the reason why!

# Eleven

# When Anne and I Are Forty-Two

## Musings of a Six-Year-Old Girl

> When Anne and I go out a walk
> We hold each other's hand and talk
> Of all the things we mean to do
> When Anne and I are forty-two.
> —A. A. Milne

We really like that poem—it's charming and not far-fetched at all, for how well we both remember something so similar when we two were six-year-olds and wondering about so many things. About the big world, and grown-ups, and growing up, and of all things—just how we'd look and be when we were forty! Martha's delightful and charming Aunt Bebe had given her some dangly earrings of hers, which gave Martha instant adulthood and utter sophistication when she chanced to put them on.

177

*I would sit with my butcher boy bobbed hair and bangs and my dangly earrings in front of the dresser mirror, and because I truly felt wise and altogether with-it, I would talk to my glorious reflection about all sorts of things—very wise things—always with the nodding agreement and accompaniment of my earrings. Why, I thought a woman with dangly earrings was automatically wise and superclass. I loved those sessions when I pondered such deep things—the ultimate one being what I'd look and be like when I was forty! Somehow that was the magic age of superwomanhood to me!*

Well, here we are writing these words and thinking once again of what the world will be like, but now what it will be like when our daughters, Lisa and Berkley, are forty or forty-two. We sometimes think we both would like those earrings to make us feel as wise as we should be, but experience has gently taught us to trade them in for strong inner values where wisdom really lies after all. Really now, what kind of world are we women letting "happen" today? We have wondered if sometimes we are too often in the business of "letting it happen" instead of building a grand place and *making* it happen. Too many people with greatness in their bones and goodness in their heart feel they're too few and far between to make a real difference in today's complex world. Not so. Cream rises, still, if it's not so homogenized that it's indistinguishable. And it makes more than a little difference. In fact, we believe that world is exactly the same as it has always been in its needs of the heart, don't you? So what kind of world is happening? It's not all good—nor is it ever all bad. Most every woman *knows* and cherishes some lasting, never-changing values she wants *always* to be recognized in her and her children's world. She may feel that lots of good things are being trampled on and she wonders if she's the only one who cares. She's *really* concerned that life's *real* foundations remain steadfast, and she's ready to be heard if she can only feel she has a chance. We've strongly felt this and have been assured over and over that so many women feel this very same way today.

Right here, we want to affirm in the strongest way that women who feel this way about these moral absolutes and ideals are *really* the majority. Women who still feel and value virtues very keenly, women who still sense and value right and wrong, women who wonder if they're the only ones left feeling that way— they're the *majority*. And they're standing up! We're seeing it happen. "Acting" cold, hard, and tough these days seems to be the "in" thing for some women, but a lot of it *is* "acting," and they're really denying their birthright, their natural grace. If strong, warm, graceful femininity is once again highly honored in our world, we'll see women taking to it like fish to water. It's their God-given nature—they'll confidently flourish. And may we say men will confidently become strong men again. Both men and women will really know who they are and how marvelously gifted God made them each. We want our daughters to grow up loving being women, honoring it, in fact. So far, so good—and it'll always be as long as we women are honorable.

We both are amazed at the similar train of thought running in women's minds today—women who are of all different backgrounds. Jung said that there is a collective unconscious that is amazingly similar and strong in the area of sensing morals. This is not to be ignored, for its power is overwhelming for

179

change in the world. To us, it is God speaking His people to action. Feel some great moral principle long enough, feel you have company in this cause, and you'll come out in the open to proclaim it. Too often, the loud voices forced upon us today as authorities are not majorities or authorities—just loud and spotlighted. Most women know the difference, and most of the time they go right on all the while ignoring these self-styled speakers for "all" women. No one guards your integrity but you. If you don't like what's being perpetrated in the name of you and your sex—stand *up*. Quietness is charming *only* if it is not really a cop-out in disguise.

What is it that's happening that most women know is bad? Really, it revolves around those two extremes we've referred to. It's this redefining of women by brash, stern women who seemingly don't like men, yet want to be like them. That's one extreme. And also, at the other extreme, an image is being conveyed that to be feminine, a woman has to be bland, pallid, weak, subservient, and have very little to do with things outside the home. The voices on each end of the spectrum give the impression that it is one alternative or the other. We don't want to be manly and crude or fakely submissive and weak—not at all. Most women like being women and like their men to be strong men, which happens in response to a strong woman. Most women we know enjoy being feminine and do not see it as one bit weak or unchallenging but plenty strong and able to accomplish anything! We were amazed to see and hear on television a prominent leader of the women's liberation movement lament, and we really mean lament: "Men just couldn't possibly know what it's been like to walk around as a woman for the last twenty-five years." She was almost teary. Our first thought was that we couldn't know about walking in men's shoes, either. We and many other women pull away from such a "female chauvinistic" attitude, for chauvinism works both ways, you know? In fact, we have talked with countless women—none of whom is uninvolved, unintelligent, or complacent—who have never felt the need to be liberated from anything; in fact, they don't identify with what the fuss is all about. So there's a lot of ambivalence: They feel maybe they ought to care, but really aren't much motivated; they're happy being women, feel quite liberated inside—and always have! No, we really don't think men are always trying to see how they can put women down or even knowing quite what to think about women today; we think men are simply confused as to their own roles in this age and we think that's understandable.

We hope our girls are their own person and understand fully what these "extremes" mean—and *never* let any group try to control them. When you're happy being a woman, you resent the voices that misrepresent womanhood to the world. No man *ever* put women down as much as women have themselves. Martha's nineteen-year-old son, Steve, brought this to our attention one day when he said how much he really respected women and couldn't understand why some of them put themselves down so much. He discerningly pointed out that their very language "being equal to men" revealed that they felt inferior of their own accord and he wasn't the only guy who saw this attitude. Every sensible woman knows that she is a dynamic, independent individual, and resents words being put in her mouth. When our girls are forty-two, will women be allowed the power and charm of their individuality? Oh, we hope so! Maybe it will be so, if we're genuinely strong and positive now, and we realize that neither aggressiveness nor passivity equals real femininity. The confident, *Christian liberated woman* doesn't need either distortion. We want Berkley's and Lisa's world to allow them to develop joyfully their own identity with no one trying to mold them into being what they think they should be. With God's help, they'll be strong to know. And their "dangly" earrings will have been exchanged for the wisdom of "knowing thyself" through the Lord.

Oh, yes, and we hope their world will be blessed with more doers than critics. We seem to be plagued now with judgers. Those who, as one person described a critic, "know the way but can't drive the car." We all do need wise counsel, but constant harsh judgment paralyzes. You seldom read a newspaper or turn on the television that someone's not berating something or someone. Some of us get hostile or indifferent when we need so desperately to get helpful. We read not long ago about the two men who were in one end of a lifeboat in the midst of a stormy sea, watching the folks at the other end of the boat desperately bailing water. One man said to the other: "Thank goodness, the hole isn't in our end of the boat!" We're all in that boat and we will share in the sinking of that boat if everybody doesn't pitch in and help. There are very few problems these days that don't affect all of us in this big boat called the world!

We *can* help the best flourish if it's nourished. No doubt about it. We have the choice. Jesus said, and we keep repeating, "Where our treasure is—our heart is also." May our treasures be reexamined seriously and changed if necessary to cure our many heart troubles. We need a new kind of heart tremor—a new look and love of those values that really touch us and make our hearts warm and make us better people. Such a thing was charmingly described by a woman in an article we read recently. Her husband's heart, seriously attacked by all its enemies, had led him to the coronary intensive care unit of a local hospital. His wife was very concerned for his every mood and feeling, because he had had such a serious heart attack and things looked rather bleak. He received, when he was able, many, many cards and letters of love and concern and good warm wishes. Reading them he began to cry; his wife seeing his tears rushed to his side. He said, "Don't worry, dear, this is a different kind of heart seizure." Yes, a different kind of heart seizure—just as real, but health-giving! And when our hearts are right, we'll be doers—truly. Love in our hearts gets translated into action; it's never static, it's not a vague platitude. No way. In fact, it is a verb.

It's happening lots today. And we hope lots when our girl's grow up. People are getting right, and setting things straight with the Lord God—*God who is love*—and it brings glory all around! As Paul said, "Christ in me—the hope of glory." If you had the spirit of Babe Ruth within you—what a great baseball player you'd be! The spirit of Abraham Lincoln—what a great statesman! The spirit of Columbus—what a great explorer! This can't happen, but *you can* have the Spirit of Christ! He's promised it for "whosoever will"—and what a great lover of mankind you'll be! It's miraculous and REAL! "Doers of the word and not hearers only"—Jesus pleaded for more of these and we so hope that when our girls are forty-two, there will be multitudes of doers, and multitudes of women doers who will "glory up" this world instead of knocking it. And we pray that Lisa and Berkley will be right there in the forefront!

One thing we know, the home will surely be strong and securely rooted when Berkley and Lisa are all grown-up, because if it has collapsed so will the world have done so. We just hope there are active people around then to keep on protecting and perpetuating the strength of the home. It seems always to need and have champions, for the forces of evil, and they're around, generation after generation, want always to stamp out these things that hold the world together. Strange that they sense the power here of the home. Who's going to be its prime champion? Who has always been? Who's made for such a divine challenge? Who knows it best? *Women.* Every woman knows this—*still!*

We simply hope our daughters will realize their full potential—everything they feel God wants and made them to be! And at this point, let us really stress some *good* things that women have going for them today. It is being revealed how talented and worthy women are in their fields of endeavor and that they deserve equal pay for equal work if they choose to or must work. How could anyone disagree with that? Wages should never be withheld for any reason—color, race, sex, religion, or whatever. In this area and so many others, surely we're growing up—and growing pains have been and are being experienced. Revolutionary growing pains, really. We women are "eyeing" one another and this suspicion is fanned and inflamed because, as Roger Williams once wrote in *Saturday Review*, one extreme "sees American women as an emerging force destined to participate as a full partner in the business of running a social system; in the partnership all distinctions establishing or even implying male supremacy will be obliterated. This *is* revolution, for at the other pole are vast multitudes of women who, while welcoming more opportunities for women and a growing appreciation of their home-oriented world, are repelled and worried by a broad-scale attack on the traditional relationship of the sexes."

This confrontation is real and it is one reason why thinking of our daughters' forty-second year is not so comfortably predictable as was our own. How will it all come out? How long will tension and divisions last? When will calm, strong voices of assurance be heard in the land instead of the harsh or weak and phony? Most of us are right in the middle trying to contribute a necessary balance—in no way complacent but, in the most basic sense, honestly confident as women. We want the same for our daughters. Fulfilled women or women comfortable with themselves can sense the flaws in the extremes, yet they'd like to help encourage the best in both areas, for both have some merit and strengths, but in a revolution, these women wonder if a third point of view can rise to the top! If fulfilled women and all the rest of us can only realize that the third point of view is really the hidden majority, what a comfort and challenge that would be! We could feel like sharing our best ideas freely.

Women in the middle have many concerns about the women's world and are concerned that in gaining what some truly feel are advantageous and honest rights for women, the crude way it's being attempted is so downgrading to the true essense of femininity that the "baby will be thrown out with the bath water." In other words, that what will be lost if we're not careful will be more valuable than what is gained. How can we women be *sure* that in all the new and revolutionary decisions, the eternal purposes for our being on this planet will remain intact unless we stay closely and honestly in touch with our God who created us with divine intentions. We'd better not ignore this: He is for us, His purposes are grander and nobler than either extreme could ever dream of. And so the woman in the middle has much to give and no excuse for passivity, for just looking both ways, for not sharing her ideas and supporting what seems to be right, under whatever banner it flies. She has hesitated sometimes, for she refuses, and rightly so, to be typecast or coerced. Her plea to the extremes is this: "Please allow me to continue to be liberated and free and I'll support and help actively those parts of each extreme I feel are beneficial to all women. Don't type me. This I *have* and *will* resent—I *am* liberated, remember?"

If we do this conscientiously, our daughters' world, your daughter's world, your granddaughter's world will be in lovingly good hands. We, in the middle between two extremes, are a little like Lot's wife—certainly not because there's good in one direction and evil in the other, which was her problem—we are looking both forward and backward, for there's both good and wrong. We have not one, but multitudinous moral decisions to stand firm on, and we must with God's help to discern, know when to stand up, move forward or back, find the good and hold it up, decry the evil, and speak out—being anything but like a pillar of salt, which only stands to show what could have been. We are, as G. K. Chesterton said: ". . . together in this world, like people in a tiny boat on a stormy sea. We owe each other a terrible loyalty!"

So true . . . like keeping the boat afloat!

I will concern myself today with:
Refusing to waste the legacy of time's
    precious hours
by wishing things were better, but making
    them
better with what I have; Feeling thankful, and
taking time to think and pray; Resolving to
learn to improve man's lot by being the first

186

to praise, the last to criticize; Losing no
   time in fretting,
but filling the hours with worthwhile things.

We Christian liberated women who have
known of Christ's inner liberation for two thousand
years have a responsibility indeed! May we do our
very best to be calm, strong, affirming and encouraging amidst a confusion that we all have to sort out.
And may God help us—all women—to honor his amazing faith in us.

And may God help us to give our daughters the
richest of spiritual legacies . . .

*Lord, the little girl out there, running across
the lawn with bare legs and her hair flying is very special . . . because she's my daughter. She's going to
need Your strength and mine to help her through the
whole thing of growing up . . . and growing up today, when so many things are pulling for her attention.*

*She's so carefree now, and I don't want her to
lose that spontaneous and uncomplicated joy that
makes her such a joy to me. But I have to teach her,
with Your help, about what lies ahead. She'll be a
grown-up woman before I know it. She'll be making
her own decisions and her own mistakes . . . and
finding that life is far from uncomplicated for a
woman.*

*I've tried so hard to give her a foundation of
faith and common sense. I want her to have a fulfilled
life, I want her to have the same kind of loving marriage that I've had. I want her to be whatever she
feels You want for her. But I know I can't take out*

187

insurance. I can only pray that she'll find as much satisfaction in being a woman, a wife, and a mother as I have . . . and that she'll know she can turn to You when she's troubled or alone . . . or joyful!

I know, Lord, that I'm praying the prayer of every mother of every daughter. But my daughter is special—because she's mine. She's myself as I once was, unformed and innocent, freckled, with a scraped knee, and full of femininity. I know the path that's ahead of her, and I know I can't travel it with her. I can only watch and sometimes call out to warn her or encourage her.

I pray that she will have all the blessings of life and the Spirit as I have had, and will thank You for them and for her womanhood, as I do.

In the name of Christ, whose love lifted us into the greatest liberation of all, thank You!

# Twelve

# You Can Go Home Again!

## Dedicated to You Who Feel the Need

When Thomas Wolfe wrote *You Can't Go Home Again*, all at once it seemed frighteningly true, yet a persistent challenge to negate. He interfered with our deep feelings about "Home," and we agreed and didn't agree all at the same time. We seemed to resent his telling us something that very personal about "our" home. Home holds for each of us some sort of meaning that's uniquely ours to look back upon or relish in the present. And though home means to each of us different things—the basic one, of course, is that it's *ours*. And we resent anyone telling us we can't go back there. Even if our home was or is not all it should be, we still resent the choice to go there being taken from us.

Why is this? Isn't it really because home is essentially *us*, and not a place? In this sense in which

189

Thomas Wolfe speaks of home as a return to a place, or youth, or simplicity, or days of growing up, or reexperiencing innocence, he's probably right, but in a much grander sense he's wrong. You *can* go home again!

You *can* because the home we're talking about is not a framework of wood and bricks and mortar, but that ideal spiritual framework of which we've spoken, of contentment and joy out of which you can function to your highest and best. You really can. It's where you're completely secure. But this home is a home that can never be confused with material ones, for it's that grand and glorious place within you— "made possible by your personal Builder." An "at home" feeling anywhere in any situation is always yours when you're honestly "at home" and comfortable with the Lord. Then happiness is within you and it's not dependent on the circumstances and surroundings alone.

Why are we saying this? Simply because we have a feeling that some one of you reading this book might have felt that you've either ignored or fled spiritual things so long and so far that you're sort of "free-floating"—not touching bottom. You're weary, tired, and you wonder if you can return at all to a "new beginning." And way down deep where no one knows but you, you *really* want that "peace that passes all understanding." Or even maybe you're reading this and you honestly wonder if you have ever known any spiritual verities, when you as a woman do *still* know you've got to function on a higher plane than the temporal to be honestly fulfilled and liberated. Who knows your heart or your thoughts? Certainly we're not claiming such insight, but we do claim as human beings to have walked down that path of sensing spiritual need, and we do claim much love and concern for each of you who read this book. You do us an honor and present us a challenge indeed. So we'd like to shout it if only we could that God loves each of you as though you were the only one to love! He made you nobly and majestically to allow Him to take up residence in your heart—to be "at home" with Him. Think of it! How more secure could you ever feel than to have such warm, comfortable communion with the Creator of everything—the Beginning and the End. Dear friend, dear reader, this is your personal God-given privilege, your right, and your ever-open door to coming home again—or even for the first time!

The prerequisite? An honest asking. God will do the rest.

Happy Homecoming!

Come unto Me all ye who are weary and heavy-laden and I will give you rest.

—Jesus

# ABOUT THE AUTHORS

MILDRED COOPER is the wife of Kenneth H. Cooper, M.D., founder of the Aerobics movement. With Dr. Cooper, she wrote *Aerobics for Women*. She has lectured to women's groups across the country and around the world on the benefits of Aerobics exercise. She was born in a small town in Oklahoma, and has two children, Berkley and Tyler. She and Dr. Cooper belong to Reverend Criswell's Baptist congregation in Dallas.

MARTHA FANNING is the wife of Buckner Fanning, Pastor of the Trinity Baptist Church of San Antonio, Texas. Buckner is the author of several religious books. Martha is a professional religious singer, whose records have sold millions of copies.

# Heartwarming Books
## of
# Faith and Inspiration

| | | | |
|---|---|---|---|
| ☐ | 11710 | **THE GOSPEL ACCORDING TO PEANUTS**<br>Robert L. Short | $1.50 |
| ☐ | 2576 | **HOW CAN I FIND YOU, GOD?**<br>Marjorie Holmes | $1.75 |
| ☐ | 10947 | **THE FINDING OF JASPER HOLT**<br>Grace Livingston Hill | $1.50 |
| ☐ | 10176 | **THE BIBLE AS HISTORY**  Werner Keller | $2.50 |
| ☐ | 12218 | **THE GREATEST MIRACLE IN THE WORLD**<br>Og Mandino | $1.95 |
| ☐ | 12009 | **THE GREATEST SALESMAN IN THE WORLD**<br>Og Mandino | $1.95 |
| ☐ | 12330 | **I'VE GOT TO TALK TO SOMEBODY, GOD**<br>Marjorie Holmes | $1.95 |
| ☐ | 12853 | **THE GIFT OF INNER HEALING**<br>Ruth Carter Stapleton | $1.95 |
| ☐ | 12444 | **BORN AGAIN**  Charles Colson | $2.50 |
| ☐ | 11012 | **FASCINATING WOMANHOOD**  Helen Andelin | $1.95 |
| ☐ | 13077 | **TWO FROM GALILEE**  Marjorie Holmes | $2.25 |
| ☐ | 12717 | **LIGHTHOUSE**  Eugenia Price | $1.95 |
| ☐ | 12835 | **NEW MOON RISING**  Eugenia Price | $1.95 |
| ☐ | 13003 | **THE LATE GREAT PLANET EARTH**<br>Hal Lindsey | $2.25 |
| ☐ | 11140 | **REFLECTIONS ON LIFE AFTER LIFE**<br>Dr. Raymond Moody | $1.95 |

**Buy them at your local bookstore or use this handy coupon for ordering:**

# MS READ-a-thon–
## a simple way
## to start youngsters reading.

Boys and girls between 6 and 14 can join the MS READ-a-thon and help find a cure for Multiple Sclerosis by reading books. And they get two rewards — the enjoyment of reading, and the great feeling that comes from helping others.

Parents and educators: For complete information call your local MS chapter, or call toll-free (800) 243-6000. Or mail the coupon below.

# Kids can help, too!